Dreams, Doubts & Determination

ENCOURAGEMENT FOR THE FAITH-BASED WRITER

Dreams, Doubts & Determination
Encouragement for the Faith-based Writer

Compiled by the KPC Writers Group
Copyright © September 24, 2024

All work is original. No AI was used. All rights reserved. No part of this publication, either text or image, may be used for any purpose other than personal use. Therefore, reproduction, modification, storage in a retrieval system, or retransmission in any form or by any means, electronic, mechanical, or otherwise, for reasons other than personal use, except for brief quotations for reviews or articles and promotion, is strictly prohibited without prior written permission by the publisher.

Edited by
Evelyn J. Wagoner, Pam Piccolo, Karen McSpadden, Jayne Ormerod

Cover Design by Valerie Fay

Graphic Design by Rachel Lyons Plumley

Original photography by DM Frech. Thanks to artist Kevin Carden.

Scripture quotations marked (KJV) are taken from the King James Version (public domain).
Scripture taken from the New King James Version® marked (NKJV). Copyright © 1982 by Thomas Nelson. Used by permission. All rights reserved.
Scripture quotations marked (NIV) are taken from the Holy Bible, New International Version®, NIV®. Copyright © 1973, 1978, 1984, 2011 by Biblica, Inc.™ Used by permission of Zondervan. All rights reserved worldwide. www.zondervan.com The "NIV" and "New International Version" are trademarks registered in the United States Patent and Trademark Office by Biblica, Inc.™
Scripture quotations marked (NIrV) are taken from the Holy Bible, New International Reader's Version®, NIrV®. Copyright © 1995, 1996, 1998, 2014 by Biblica, Inc.™ Used by permission of Zondervan. All rights reserved worldwide. www.zondervan.com The "NIrV" and "New International Reader's Version" are trademarks registered in the United States Patent and Trademark Office by Biblica, Inc.™
Scripture quotations marked (MSG) are taken from THE MESSAGE. Copyright © 1993, 1994, 1995, 1996, 2000, 2001, 2002. Used by permission of NavPress Publishing Group.
Scripture quotations taken from the (NASB®) New American Standard Bible®, Copyright © 1960, 1971, 1977, 1995 by The Lockman Foundation. Used by permission. All rights reserved. lockman.org
Scripture quotations taken from the Amplified® Bible (AMP), Copyright © 2015 by The Lockman Foundation. Used by permission. lockman.org
Scripture quotations taken from the Amplified® Bible (AMPC), Copyright © 1954, 1958, 1962, 1964, 1965, 1987 by The Lockman Foundation. Used by permission. lockman.org
Scripture quotations marked (ASV) are taken from the American Standard Version (public domain).
Scripture quotations marked (NLT) are taken from the Holy Bible, New Living Translation. Copyright © 1996, 2004, 2015 by Tyndale House Foundation. Used by permission of Tyndale House Publishers, Carol Stream, Illinois 60188, USA. All rights reserved.
The Holy Bible, Berean Standard Bible, (BSB) is produced in cooperation with Bible Hub, Discovery Bible, OpenBible.com, and the Berean Bible Translation Committee. This text of God's Word has been dedicated to the public domain.
Scripture quotations marked (CSB) have been taken from the Christian Standard Bible®, Copyright © 2017 by Holman Bible Publishers. Used by permission. Christian Standard Bible® and CSB® are federally registered trademarks of Holman Bible Publishers.
Scripture quotations marked (NRSV) are taken from the New Revised Standard Version Bible: Anglicized Edition. Copyright © 1989, 1995 National Council of the Churches of Christ in the United States of America. Used by permission. All rights reserved worldwide.

ISBN 979-8-9913578-0-7

Published by
MAN IN THE MIDDLE PRESS, LLC
A Bridge Between Writers and Readers • Linking Goals to Grace

VIRGINIA BEACH, VA

With gratitude to our Lord and Savior,
Jesus Christ,
the Author and Finisher of our faith,

and

Reverend Neil Ellison.
Your writer's heart never failed to
encourage and support us.
Because of you, we are a family.

Dreams, Doubts & Determination

Encouragement for the Faith-based Writer

Compiled by the KPC Writers Group

Published by

MAN IN THE MIDDLE PRESS, LLC

A Bridge Between Writers and Readers • Linking Goals to Grace

VIRGINIA BEACH, VA

We use our powerful God-tools for smashing warped philosophies, tearing down barriers erected against the truth of God, fitting every loose thought and emotion and impulse into the structure of life shaped by Christ. Our tools are ready at hand for clearing the ground of every obstruction and building lives of obedience into maturity.

2 Corinthians 10:4b-6 (MSG)

For the weapons of our warfare are not carnal but mighty in God for pulling down strongholds, casting down arguments and every high thing that exalts itself against the knowledge of God, bringing every thought into captivity to the obedience of Christ, and being ready to punish all disobedience when your obedience is fulfilled.

2 Corinthians 10:4-6 (NKJV)

Contents

FOREWORD Rev. Neil Ellison i
INTRODUCTION Pam Piccolo iii

Welcome

A CALLING TO WRITE Jennifer Napier 2
LONG ROAD BEHIND Karen McSpadden 5
A WRITER'S PRAYER Joyce Hammer 6

Part 1: Dreams

HEARTBURN & LOVE STORIES Evelyn J. Wagoner 10
A WRITER'S PRAYER Lori Higgins 12
THE DREAM Kathy Daugherty 13
MILESTONE MOMENTS Valerie Fay 14
A WRITER'S PRAYER Samuel Frech 15
A VOW OF SURRENDER AMIDST THE STORM Lori Higgins 16

Gifts

A CALL TO YOUR CALLING Karen McSpadden 20
WRITING FOR THE GLORY OF GOD Joyce Kirby 23
HONE YOUR CRAFT Joyce Hammer 25
A WRITER'S PRAYER Sherry Elliott 27
WE HAVE THE LIGHT Patti Jarrett 28
A WRITER'S PRAYER Joyce Kirby 30
MORE THAN TECHNICIANS Pam Piccolo 31

Unique Voice

WRITING UNDER THE INFLUENCE Jayne Ormerod 36
DROWNING IDENTITY Amy Heilman 38
A WRITER'S PRAYER Dr. James R. Boyd 40

RELUCTANT WRITER	*Julie Strohkorb*	41
THE FABRIC OF LIFE	*Valerie Fay*	43
BE STILL AND KNOW	*Amy Heilman*	45
HEARING THE VOICE	*Dr. James R. Boyd*	46
THE GIFT IN THE VOICES	*Sherry Elliott*	48
A WRITER'S PRAYER	*Benton Hammond*	50

Story

IT IS WRITTEN	*Kathy Daugherty*	56
WHO ARE YOU AND WHO ARE YOU IN CHRIST	*DM Frech*	59
A WRITER'S PRAYER	*Joyce Hammer*	61
LOST IN TRANSLATION	*Pam Piccolo*	62
THIS MOMENT	*Kathy Daugherty*	64

Unique Message

NO LONGER SELF-EVIDENT	*Pam Piccolo*	68
JESUS FIRE	*Eileen Frost*	70
THE WORD OF THEIR TESTIMONY	*Derick Carstens*	71
A WRITER'S PRAYER	*Amy Heilman*	73
WHEREVER HE LEADS	*Sherry Elliott*	74
A WRITER'S PRAYER	*Derick Carstens*	77
A PROVOCATEUR FOR LOVE	*Steven Webber*	78
CITY ON A HILL	*Elizabeth Green*	81
EVERYDAY MIRACLES	*Pam Piccolo*	82
TO CARRY THE LIGHT	*Valerie Fay*	84

Part 2: DOUBTS

THE MINISTRY OF LISTENING	*Evelyn J. Wagoner*	88
CONFESSIONS OF A FEAR-BASED WRITER	*Yvonne Saxon*	91
RUN TO THE LION	*Jessica Snook*	92
WHO I AM MEANT TO BE	*Lori Higgins*	94
A WRITER'S PRAYER	*Merle Mills*	97
H-A-P-P-Y	*Karen McSpadden*	98
WHEN DOUBT CREEPS IN	*Penny Hutson*	101

THE BATTLE WITHIN	Lori Higgins	103
CREATIVE BEAUTY	Merle Mills	105
IS ANYBODY OUT THERE?	Merle Mills	106
GO AHEAD AND QUIT	John Reddel	107

Vulnerability

GOD'S HEART	Rachel Plumley	112
ODE TO THE ARTIST	Jessica Snook	114
ECHOES OF ETERNITY	Lori Higgins	116
A WRITER'S PRAYER	Rachel Plumley	117
ME OVER HERE, YOU OVER THERE	Benton Hammond	118
BRISK AND SUNNY	DM Frech	121

Healing

LIVING A DREAM, WAKING UP TO REALITY	Valerie Fay	126
I'LL TAKE SPRINKLES	Eileen Frost	129
WELCOMED INTO HEALING	Rachel Plumley	130
A WRITER'S PRAYER	Jennifer Napier	132

Part 3: DETERMINATION

A VIRTUAL SLAP FOR THE BOGEYMAN	Evelyn J. Wagoner	136
DYING	DM Frech	139
HE KNEW THE COCK WOULD CROW	Jessica Snook	140
SONG TO THE WEARY	Jessica Snook	142
A LESSON IN LOVE AND DETERMINATION	Billie Montgomery/Cook	144
PSALM OF TRUST	Amy Heilman	148
PERSEVERANCE IN THE MIDST OF REJECTION	Dr. James R. Boyd	149
A WRITER'S PRAYER	Mary Stasko	151

Process

DO THESE FOUR THINGS	Dylan West	156
GRATITUDE	Mary Stasko	161
ADVICE TO STRUGGLING WRITERS	Elizabeth Green	162

JANXIETY *Karen McSpadden*	163
A TIME FOR EVERY THING *Penny Hutson*	166
A WRITER'S PRAYER *Dylan West*	167

Responsibility

IN PLAIN SIGHT *Evelyn J. Wagoner*	172
A WRITER'S PRAYER *Valerie Fay*	174
THE CHALLENGE OF CARPE DIEM *Joyce Kirby*	175
PROCRASTINATION . . . A DISCOURSE *Derick Carstens*	177
NEXT TIME *DM Frech*	179

Excellence

LOVE YOUR READERS *Dylan West*	182
A WRITER'S PRAYER *John Reddel*	184
CONFESSIONS OF CAPTAIN OBVIOUS *Pam Piccolo*	185
WHEN GOOD ISN'T GOOD ENOUGH *Jayne Ormerod*	188
THREE THOUGHTS ON EXCELLENT WRITING *Karen McSpadden*	190

Prayer

AS YOU WRITE *Mary Stasko*	194
A WRITER'S PRAYER *Kathy Daugherty*	196
TEN DIFFERENT PLACES TO PRAY *Olivia Arney*	197
A WRITER'S WORK *Mary Stasko*	201
A WRITER'S PRAYER *Lori Higgins*	202
THE WRITER'S PSALM *Sherrie Pilkington*	206

Try Your Hand

I'M CHOOSING LIFE *Jennifer Napier*	211
SECRET THOUGHTS *Paula Grimsley*	212
THE GARDEN GATE *Ann Abraham*	213
GET BACK UP *Rachel Plumley*	214

THE MOST IMPORTANT PERSON	*Olivia Arney*	215
LALIBELA	*Dylan West*	216
SILENCE OF MY HEART	*Lori Higgins*	217
AN INAPPROPRIATE TIME TO LAUGH	*Pam Piccolo*	218
TO ALL THE SHIPS AT SEA	*Evelyn J. Wagoner*	221
SIGNPOSTS OF THE TIMES	*Ann Abraham*	222
FOG	*Dylan West*	225
DUMPSTER DIVA	*Patti Jarrett*	226
THE FALL OF MAN	*Pam Piccolo*	227
THE LAST TIME I SAW HER	*Joyce Hammer*	228
RAIN	*DM Frech*	229
THE HOLIDAY FIASCO	*Patti Jarrett*	230
WALKING IN THE WOODS	*Dylan West*	231
AMERICAN IDOL REWIND	*Pam Piccolo*	232
A HOPE FOR THE FUTURE	*Lori Higgins*	233
THE FUGITIVE & HAIKU	*Patti Jarrett*	234
SUPERHERO	*Samuel Frech*	235
FULL OF BACON	*Ed Frost*	236
BABY, IT'S COLD OUTSIDE & THE COLDEST PLACE	*Pam Piccolo*	237
RELUCTANCE	*Dylan West*	239
FROM HERE TO YESTERYEAR	*Lori Higgins*	240
FAMILY VACATION	*Patti Jarrett*	241
6-WORD MEMOIRS	*Pam Piccolo, Rachel Plumley, Eileen Frost*	242
GONE WITH THE WIND	*Ed Frost*	243
A SUDDEN SILENCE	*Benton Hammond*	244
DEAR YOUNGER ME	*Rachel Plumley*	246
VENTIFACTS	*Dylan West*	247
JUST THE FACTS	*Patti Jarrett*	248
ON A JUNE NIGHT	*Karen McSpadden*	249
BEAUTY TRIUMPHS	*Ed Frost*	250

About the Authors ... 251

Acknowledgements ... 289

Foreword

Have you ever thought, "I would love to become a writer. Wouldn't it be great to write a book and have it published? But who would ever want to read what I write? I can't be a writer!"

Twenty years ago, when I was serving as a Congregational Care Pastor, my duties included overseeing Small Group Ministries. A staff member asked if I would support her in starting a writers group. I responded, "Only if you hold it on a night when I can attend!" Because of the KPC Writers Group, I became a writer.

The important part of this story is that I have never had a book published, yet I call myself a writer. When I am introduced to people, they may ask what I do. I might respond, "Among other things, I am a writer." My identity as a writer is not because I have published works, but because I write. That's what writers do. They write.

My hope and prayer for you is that this anthology, *Dreams, Doubts & Determination: Encouragement for the Faith-based Writer,* will inspire you to become the writer you were meant to be. As you read, set a specific time each day to sit down with paper and pencil. Set a timer for two minutes and start writing. (Of course, you can write longer than two minutes, but it's a start.) And may you, too, experience the joy of becoming a Writer.

Rev. Neil Ellison
Pastor of Congregational Care, Retired (*and a writer*)

Introduction

Great things can emerge through casual conversation. Alexander Graham Bell's comment, "Mr. Watson, come here. I want to see you," expressed over his newly invented telephone, advanced communication considerably. Had Watson not clearly heard and responded, we might still rely on the Pony Express to get our messages across.

What if Benjamin Franklin had never engaged in debate over the nature of lightning? Hypothetically, we'd still be in the dark! Like electricity, bright ideas are truly discovered more than invented. God creates the energy. We employ the spark.

Such ideas rarely come from working in isolation, but more so from unplanned chats outside the laboratory or lecture hall. Each person holds part of the story. Creativity blossoms with shared experience.

So it was, in 2004, when across the pews of Kempsville Presbyterian Church, a random notion found fertile ground. Writers were there, itching to write. But without the encouragement of community, we were at a loss for words. Like our Creator, our thoughts needed outlet via the expressed word to become real. The KPC Writers Group began in response to this need and, with the Lord's blessing, still flourishes.

God, through the Holy Spirit, uses human words to reveal His character and Truth. Our desire to affirm our God-given passion to write by faithfully developing skill, kindling creativity, and setting reachable goals has resulted in this anthology. We invite you, regardless of skill level, experience, age, or genre, to join us in this humble endeavor. We earnestly hope our essays, poems, prayers, and guided journaling will embolden each faith-based writer to wholeheartedly follow our gift-giving God and spread the word!

Pam Piccolo
KPC Writers Group Founding Member

All writing comes
by the grace of God.
RALPH WALDO EMERSON

Photography by DM Frech

WELCOME

*The words of the godly
encourage many.*
Proverbs 10:21a (NLT)

A Calling to Write

Jennifer Napier

There is something inside us that inherently connects with words. With stories. With creating. With imagining. With dreaming. With remembering. With processing. With learning. With researching. We have found that we come alive when we write. We are stirred to write. Compelled to write. Gifted to write. This is something God has placed within us. If I may be so bold, *we are called to write*.

Maybe your writing began when you were young. Maybe it was something you came upon more recently. Maybe it's been a stumbling, wandering process. Or maybe you've always felt connected when your hand puts pen or pencil to paper or your fingers stroke the keys of your word processor.

Writing is not for the faint of heart. It draws on our emotions and feelings and takes us places we don't want to go. It unburies hurts and draws up wells of old, painful, broken stories. It casts characters we become too attached to. It causes us to pull our words back from others afraid of how they would respond if they really knew how we felt, who we were, what we lacked. But here, in this safe place, in this shelter for writers, let me ask . . .

Who here is tired? Who is weary? Who here is burnt out? Are you broken? Struggling? Exhausted? Do you feel insufficient? Incapable? Not enough? Too much? Torn? Bedraggled? Grief stricken? Lonely? Empty?

Let us draw near to the well, to the One who never runs dry. Though we pant with desire, He will satisfy the deepest longings of our hearts. His power is made present, made manifest, shows up, and shows off in our weakness. Run to Him. Author of life. Perfecter of our selves. Redeemer and Savior who has rescued us. We don't have to do more or be more to be loved. Come with open hands, ready to receive. Ready to taste and see that the Lord is good. We would have despaired had we not believed that we would see the goodness of the Lord in the land of the living.

In the land of the living, even if we pass through the valley of the shadow of death, we will fear no evil. Your rod and staff comfort us. You lead us in pastures that are green and lush, full of provision. You protect us from the cliffs that we wander too close to. You direct us to still waters so that we are not sucked into the current. We will not be pulled under and drowned. Your paths for us are life. Nourishment. Fulfillment. Hope and joy. Our future is bright when we look to You. When we look away from the storms that threaten to cause despair. When we look up to You and we see that we are held in a hand that can never be shaken. We are held by the One who created the sun and put the planets in orbit. Who knows the galaxies and calls each star by name. Who set the galaxies in their boundary lines and created force and motion. Who subdues tidal waves. Who releases the pressure of volcanoes. Who calms the storms of the raging seas and of our raging hearts.

Oh, writer, take courage and take heart. Your writing is for you, but not just for you. It's for your edification but not merely your own edification. As we lean into the Lord and are filled with His Spirit, we are enabled to be more than we are. We are a conduit of blessing. Our stories bring healing. Our words bring life. We are people who give joy and laughter. We give comfort to those in sorrow. We bring delight in anecdotes. We offer encouragement, direction, and moments of transcendence . . . a reminder that this world is not our final home. Our words direct contemplation. Our words remind. Our words teach and instruct. Our words reveal patterns and habits and cycles. Our words bring connection. Our words bring healing. Our words add humor. Our words honor and shine light.

Our stories remind others they are not alone. They allow others to have words for their very real feelings and experiences and give language where there was only muteness. They create songs for those who were deaf and sight for those who were blind. We are transporters of time and space and other realms. We are light givers for those stumbling on the path.

In this gifting, this talent with words, this deep emotion and expression that has been nestled so deep inside of us is placed a calling. One that has been instilled by God and that passion and gifting becomes a place of blessing for others.

We do this not in our own strength. But in the strength of the creator of all. The One who established time and space and being. Who chose us before time. Who created us to be word-wielders and story tellers and hope dealers.

Gather round. Take heart. Press in. As you lean into your words, know these words aren't your own. They are for more than our own pleasure. So, we respond with pen and pencil and laptop in hand. With every flourish of our writing instrument or every tapping of keys may we feel the pleasure of knowing we are doing what were created for. We are fulfilling the purpose for which we have been called.

My dear ones, the best is yet to come.

Long Road Behind

Long road behind, long road ahead.
Bitter winter, weary land.

The Word still burns,
stubborn-bright light for the path.
The Spirit hovers, still forming
my formless heart.
God still is my portion,
Christ my consolation.
Oh to enter His rest—but not yet.
Let me enter exhausted and spent,
worn and weather-beaten.
Let me enter with nothing but Him
and I enter with all things.

Long road behind, long road ahead
Bright the stars, bright our joy.

I lift up mine eyes.

Karen McSpadden

A Writer's Prayer

Heavenly Father, as I sit down to write today, I confess that I believe Your Word is true, and You will assist me to write what You want me to write.

Lord God, I offer myself to You *a living sacrifice, holy and acceptable* because of the blood of Christ. (Romans 12:1)

Thank You that You who began a good work in me will complete it. (Philippians 1:6)

Thank You for calling me to write for You. You are faithful and will do it through me. (1 Thessalonians 5:24)

Thank You that, as I trust in You and acknowledge You in all my ways, You will direct my path. (Proverbs 3:5-6)

Thank You that I am one of Your sheep. I hear Your voice, and I follow You. (John 10:27)

Thank You for assisting me with Your ministering angels, who excel in strength and heed the voice of Your Word. (Psalm 103:20)

Your Word shall not return to You void, but it shall accomplish what You please. (Isaiah 55:11)

I will praise You, for I am fearfully and wonderfully made. (Psalm 139:14 NKJV)

I am complete in You. (Colossians 2:10)

Your grace is sufficient for me. (2 Corinthians 12:9)

I can do all things through Christ who strengthens me. Philippians 4:13 (NKJV)

I am excited about writing for You, because You are working in me to do Your good pleasure. (Philippians 2:13)

In Jesus' name, Amen.

Joyce Hammer

"You write to communicate to the hearts and minds of others what's burning inside you, and we edit to let the fire show through the smoke."

Arthur Plotnik

Part 1: Dreams

Oh, that my words were written!
Oh, that they were inscribed in a book!
That they were engraved on a rock
With an iron pen and lead, forever!
For I know that my Redeemer lives,
And He shall stand at last on the earth;

Job 19:23-25 (NKJV)

Heartburn & Love Stories

Evelyn J. Wagoner

I attended a "destiny" conference presented by Billy Godwin and cried because my dream was too small. As I heard the dreams of other folks, I felt myself growing smaller and smaller, disgraced by their grandness compared to mine. They wanted to use their gifts to reach orphans, businessmen, housewives, teens, etc. for Christ. Their visions were so lofty, so glorious, so, well, godly. Just listening made me shrink inside. I almost ran out the door in humiliation.

We were coached to write our personal mission statements, our visions for our lives. I sat there. Embarrassed. Mortified. Unworthy.

I wanted to write love stories. With happy endings.

Two friends hauled me up to talk to Billy. In less than sixty seconds Billy had me in tears. I can't to this day remember what he said in those moments, but in no time at all I realized that my dream was just as valid as everyone else's. And my mission statement?

As a writer, my God-given mission is to demonstrate God's steadfast devotion to us by unfolding the eternal truths of faith, hope, and love, through creative storytelling .

I try to remind myself of that. Often. But it's hard.

Recently, our pastor spoke of Jesus and the two disciples on the road to Emmaus. I love that story. Jesus suddenly appears as Cleopas and some nameless guy are walking the seven miles from Jerusalem to Emmaus. Jesus asks what they're talking about and why they look so sad. They think Jesus has to be the most clueless fellow in the country, the only one who doesn't know what's been going on. They tell Him about His own trial, death, and resurrection.

After Jesus opens the Word to them and reveals who He is, they say, *Did not our heart burn within us while He talked with us on the road, and while He opened the Scriptures to us?* (Luke 24:32b NKJV)

Jeremiah tells us of his discouragement and determination to shut up, to stop preaching, to stop proclaiming what the Lord told him to say. *But His word was in my heart like a burning fire shut up in my bones; I was weary of holding it back, and I could not.* (Jeremiah 20:9b NKJV)

Our pastor then prayed for us all to have burning hearts and reminded us that it was in the image of fire that the Holy Spirit descended at Pentecost.

I knew everyone else was thinking about being brave for Jesus, about witnessing, about impacting the world in some wonderful way. But all I could think of was how my heart used to burn with my God-given mission for writing love stories.

How easy it is to set that dream aside and do other things that play around it, that are sort of "related." How easy it is to tell myself that it's hopeless, that no one wants to read what I write, that I really have nothing to say. There's nothing in me worth pouring out.

Then I think, even if all that were true, could I ever really give up? While the flame may not always be blazing, the embers never go out. They're waiting to be breathed on, to be stirred.

"Kingdom dreams come from our broken past. What the enemy once tried to steal, God redeems." (Jennifer Wagemaker for God-sizedDreams.com)

My dream has validity even in its simplicity, though the "coming true" part is a lot more complicated. I remind myself of what Holley Gerth says: "There is a message inside you that only you can share. We don't get a second chance at it. There is no back-up plan in God's agenda. You're the world's one shot at what God has placed in you."

I feel discouragement dropping its "dis" and remember a recent comment from my friend who said, "Your life seems to be full of love stories."

He's right. It is.

And doesn't the world need more love stories?

A Writer's Prayer

LORD, You know my heart and all my desires. The longing that I have felt all my life to dream up stories and to tell them in some form. You know that I desire to hold my first book in my hands and to have that satisfaction that I never gave up, that I kept going no matter how hard it became, because I loved it.

Please help me stay motivated and to keep going. Please help me when I struggle and give me peace when I do. Help me to focus and to write the words that beg to be let out. Yet, on those hard days when I do struggle, and I don't feel the words, help me give myself some grace. A moment to breathe and to be kind to myself and to take the time to rest if needed. Then, when it's time, please help my words bloom on the page and continue to write, even when the words try to elude me.

Lori Higgins

The Dream
Kathy Daugherty

Writing was not my dream. I didn't have the faith or the confidence to dream big enough. Becoming a writer was never in my plan, for I never thought I was capable. I was nobody, and nobodies didn't accomplish anything special. We get by—something like squeaking through.

We are pretty much an invisible lot. When peers look around for someone to accomplish anything significant, they don't look in our direction. And I was not one to argue. To do that, I would have to speak up for myself. That wasn't likely to happen, for I had no voice, no goals, no expectations. I thought myself to be a barren plot of land with hopes of becoming little else.

However, there was a Gardener who had plans and dreams for this simple little plot. He tended the soil, planting seeds—knowing they would germinate at different times and that, in His perfect timing, the beginning of a garden would emerge. Little by little, tiny sprouts appeared at sparse intervals, almost undetected. The "nobody garden" began to grow, and thoughts tentatively sprouted forth like new vines.

Ultimately, the dream the Gardener had placed in me began to take shape. Words from the Lord slowly blossomed like a new bud displaying the slightest hint of color in its petals. Ever so slowly it happened. "Nobody" began to speak, to share, daring to write the words the Gardener gave her—first on little scraps of paper, then in a notebook, social media, and even in a weekly online devotional.

From the shell of a nobody, "somebody" was birthed—and a writer was created.

Milestone Moments
Valerie Fay

The plan was to drive west from my home in Virginia Beach to Wisconsin, but, after a number of hours on the road, the signpost stated Washington, DC 30 miles! It would have been insanity to continue on that same road and expect to end up at my destination.

Have you ever invested your hopes and dreams in someone or something that turned out to be contrary to the plan and purpose of God? Many have. We travel a path we're sure is God's will only to find that we must turn and move in another direction.

Have you found yourself at that place where you're asking, "How do I reconcile broken dreams with God's purpose?"

Many years ago, I received a prophetic word that seemed to reinforce a long-held desire, only to find that it didn't work out as I had expected. Scripture tells us that *we see through a glass, darkly.* (1 Corinthians 13:12) I had been looking through a distorted lens. Only God knows the end from the beginning, and sometimes we must endure seeming defeat in order to step into the glorious future God has prepared.

Only as we lay our limited understanding before the throne of an all-knowing God will we be ready to proceed along the road He has chosen we travel. There will be times when God steps in and changes the direction of our lives.

It is His prerogative; He is Lord. How we choose to respond will determine our effectiveness in His Kingdom. We may not need to have the answer to every question, but we can trust the One who is Light when our course leads through dark valleys.

It is God who holds our lives in His hands, and no weapon formed against us will prosper. (Isaiah 54:17) For any of us, life can change in an instant. There could be challenging times ahead, but each day will hold promise of a new beginning.

There must be no turning back to lesser things.

A Writer's Prayer

Heavenly Father, I pray for dreams to come true. Help me to overcome distractions and focus on reality so that I can be motivated to work past the constant writer's block that plagues me before and during my writing. Please help me make the right choices in the story I have yet to tell and prepare the way for what it may become.

In Jesus' name, Amen.

Samuel Frech

A Vow of Surrender Amidst the Storm
Lori Higgins

In the night, I gave you a name, a title, and in that moment, you came to life. A new dream was born based on all the ones that had come before. I called you mine—and a horde of fears rushed in. Much like the aftermath of birth, the quickening resumed. Flares of questions pressed harshly into the corners of my mind, breaking through my defenses. Doubts came in like a flood.

Yet, my need to show what burns in my veins carries me.

Determination is the buoy I cling to in the vast sea of apprehension that will surely pull me under. At my worst, fears cost me my grip, and I allow myself to let go. I tread against the doubts, certain I am not as good as I could be. I am all but frozen as the wind picks up. Each gale brings every harsh thought that I've ever had against myself. I still fight even as my body weakens.

As the dark waters pull me under, I let it go. I surrender to the One who created me. The One who is the Master Storyteller of all, and who knows not only the beginning but the end. He has never known a blank page in the history of time. I finally rest in Him. I hand Him each broken piece of my spirit, and a warmth of resolve breathes within that fragile cavity.

For a moment, the world is still, and then I find myself on the wet sand of the shore. It's still night, and the storm is still going strong, but I'm no longer in it. The steady glow of a lighthouse shines somewhere in the distance. I feel a promise in its ray that I am not alone and never will be.

Struggles will come and go, but we will never be alone. Sometimes we must surrender, but we cannot give up. We surrender and lay our heart before our Creator, and rest in Him. The rest of our story will continue—the one we write and the one we are living.

Questions for Guided Journaling

Have you sought the Lord for a vision for your writing? If so, are you walking in obedience to that vision?

_____
_____
_____
_____
_____
_____
_____
_____
_____
_____
_____
_____
_____
_____

Show me the path where I should walk, O Lord;
point out the right road for me to follow.
Lead me by your truth and teach me, for you are the God
who saves me. All day long I put my hope in you.
Psalms 25:4-5 (NLT)

GIFTS

For the gifts and the calling of God are irrevocable [for He does not withdraw what He has given, nor does He change His mind about those to whom He gives His grace or to whom He sends His call].

Romans 11:29 (AMP)

"The gift God has given you is not separate from His purpose for your life."
Valerie Fay

A Call to Your Calling
(Psalm 33 for Writers)
Karen McSpadden

Good people, cheer GOD!
Right-living people sound best when praising.
   Use guitars to reinforce your hallelujahs!
Play His praise on a grand piano!
Compose your own new song to Him;
   give Him a trumpet fanfare.

    Writers, bring your pens and your paper. Let your ink flow and your hearts rejoice! May the clatter of clicking keyboards chatter out a chorus to our God! Be bold! Be boisterous! Proclaim on the page the praise of our God!

For GOD's Word is solid to the core;
   everything He makes is sound inside and out.
He loves it when everything fits,
   when His world is in plumb-line true.
Earth is drenched
   in GOD's affectionate satisfaction.

    Writers, you are drenched in God's affectionate satisfaction every time you sit to write! Whether you are writing a five-minute exercise or a five-hundred-page novel, a diary or a devotional, whether you write for private goals or publication, whether you are just starting or are a seasoned craftsman, God is delighted by the sheer act of your writing. You echo His image as Creator! You capture every nook and cranny of His world!

The skies were made by GOD's command;
   He breathed the word and the stars popped out.
He scooped sea into His jug,
   put ocean in His keg.

    Writers, may your words flow! May they be broad and deep as oceans, as vast as stars! May they come forth at the command of your God, be it a trickle or a ripple or a flood. May He draw up from your soul the messages He longs to send through you.

Earth-creatures, bow before GOD;
  world-dwellers—down on your knees!
Here's why: He spoke and there it was,
  in place the moment He said so.

Writers, you were made for this! God sang over you before you were even born. In the moment He conceived of your conception, He planted this seed in your soul. Do not let anyone diminish what God has called you to be.

GOD takes the wind out of Babel pretense,
  He shoots down the world's power-schemes.
GOD's plan for the world stands up,
  all His designs are made to last.
Blessed is the country with GOD for God;
  blessed are the people He's put in His will.

Writers, God's plan for your writing will prevail. It is already complete in His mind and in His heart, and it will not fail to be completed in your life. Do not try to take over His job as script-writer. Be faithful to the work of your words, take delight in your journey, and let Him guide your steps.

From high in the skies GOD looks around,
  He sees all Adam's brood.
From where He sits
  He overlooks all us earth-dwellers.
He has shaped each person in turn;
  now He watches everything we do.

Writers, just as God has shaped you, so He sees you. He sees both the joy of your writing and the weariness, the faith and the doubt, the successes and the stumbles. He is at your side even when you sit alone at your writing desk or in the deep places of your desires, your fears, and your fatigue. His habitation is with you.

No king succeeds with a big army alone,
  no warrior wins by brute strength.
Horsepower is not the answer;
  no one gets by on muscle alone.

Writers, your own strength will not save you or sustain your stories. Study! Practice! Improve! But do not trust that for the power of your writing.

Watch this: God's eye is on those who respect Him,
  the ones who are looking for His love.
He's ready to come to their rescue in bad times;
  in lean times He keeps body and soul together.

Writers, He will hold you fast. He will come to your aid. He will keep you together even when life seems to fly apart.

We're depending on GOD;
  He's everything we need.
What's more, our hearts brim with joy
  since we've taken for our own His holy name.
Love us, GOD, with all you've got—
  that's what we're depending on. (Psalm 33 The Message)

Writers, let your hearts brim with joy. You have been given every word in every tongue for your inheritance. You have been given eternity to speak. But do not wait! Spend freely your word-hoard, because you will never reach the bottom. Speak and sing now, because you will never run out of things to say. When you think you have reached the end of your words, God will lead you into even deeper and wider places!

Yes, love us, God, with all you've got.
  Make our hearts to love You with all we've got.
Increase our trust in You,
  On and off the page.
You are everything we need.

Writing for the Glory of God
Joyce Kirby

L*et the message of Christ dwell among you richly as you teach and admonish one another with all wisdom through psalms, hymns, and songs from the Spirit, singing to God with gratitude in your hearts. And whatever you do, whether in word or deed, do it all in the name of the Lord Jesus, giving thanks to God the Father through him.* (Colossians 3:16-17 NIV)

. . . whatever you do, do it all for the glory of God. (1 Corinthians 10:31b NIV)

What do Moses, David, and Paul have in common with Augustine, Martin Luther, John Calvin, or Fanny Crosby? They were writers. Moses, David, Paul, along with many others, wrote the books of the Bible. They wrote at different times, centuries apart in some cases. They wrote in different genres: history, poetry, eyewitness testimony, and dreams. They each were inspired by the Holy Spirit and wrote to preserve God's truth as well as His redemption plan through His Son. The thread that ties them together is the same thread that ties us together.

Augustine, Martin Luther, and John Calvin wrote to help us better understand what God's Word means and how it should apply to our lives. Fanny Crosby wrote timeless hymns, many of which are still sung in churches today. And God is still gifting His people with the ability to write!

To consider that we too have a message to write for God is both a grand gift and a boundless burden. Though our message will not be canonized in another book of the Bible, it is nonetheless important because God has, indeed, gifted us and burdened our hearts to write for Him, for His glory. We have the obligation to pursue it to the best of our ability.

Writing that glorifies God takes many forms. Pastors typically write out their sermons. Various genres of song are written to teach us to know God and how to worship God. Articles and books are written to encourage us in the faith. Painters often use their brushes to "write" a message on a canvas. Regardless of the mode it takes, a believer who has this gift writes for a specific purpose in the kingdom of God—to encourage, to teach, to admonish, and to cheer using their specific talent. All this is done for the glory of God.

We have a written Bible today because those who came before us yielded themselves to the Holy Spirit and documented what the Spirit spoke through them. Their message was important and timeless and preserved through the ages. Think about that for a second! Even in that time, a time with primitive writing means at best, God inspired them then preserved His message for generations to come. God provided the message by inspiration and used ordinary, and, dare I say, flawed people like Moses, David, and Paul to distribute that message to the world. Likewise, today He is using us to tell our own part of His story in our own special way.

So, what are we to do with our gift? We must diligently pursue our writing in praise and prayer with thanksgiving, seeking God's wisdom for what He wants us to write. Don't hide it under a bushel! Writing is the way God has given you to shine for Him! You may not see the whole picture because that is not God's purpose for you. You are to faithfully write and seek God's direction and God will work out everything else. The results are His.

Do you think Moses, David, Paul, and all the others ever conceived that their writings would be gathered into an anthology that has survived the ages and now is available, not on a scroll but in book form, mass produced and online, in various translations and languages? I think not! We may never realize on this side of eternity why God has gifted us in this way. We don't need to. He knows! We just need to embrace our gift, seek His guidance, invite His inspiration and, as we are led, we are to write, write, write—all for the glory of God.

Hone Your Craft
Joyce Hammer

I never considered myself to be a writer. I'm the person who takes copious notes. Except for writing letters and writing in my journal, I never liked to write. It was hard for me to come up with ideas and outlines.

My friend Judy needed an editor for her book, so I volunteered. When we finished, she said God told her we were supposed to do something together. She wouldn't tell me what, as she wanted God to tell me. I was excited that God wanted us to do something together, but I didn't have any idea what it might be, and I didn't want to try to figure it out. I wanted God to tell me.

In a dream, He showed me I was to go to a women's conference and receive prayer. God imparted something to me that day. As I dusted our bookshelves a few days later, I suddenly *knew* Judy and I were to write a book together. I assumed she would write and I would edit, as we did before. That was not the case. God wanted us to write the book together.

Shortly afterwards, I began attending the KPC Writers Group. It was helpful and fun, however, when we read our writing prompts, the others sounded polished and creative. Mine sounded plain and lifeless. Clearly, I was not in their league. I felt like a kindergartener in a graduate class.

Nevertheless, Judy and I wrote chapters in our book. We got off to a good start, but as time went on, I gradually questioned God calling me to write. I procrastinated, waiting for God to drop an idea into my head.

A few years later, I began working full time and dropped out of the Writers Group. I said I was too tired to attend the meetings. I was tired, but that was just an excuse.

One night in a dream, I heard the words, "Hone your craft." Although the words sounded strange to me, I instinctively knew exactly what God was saying. He wanted me to develop my writing skills and finish the book.

A couple of days later, while deleting unread emails, I noticed one from a woman who leads a writers conference each year in Philadelphia. I scanned it, and—right in the middle of the email—words popped off the page: "Hone your craft." What a surprise!

A confirmation! In addition, she wrote that it was important for a writer to be in a writers group. That settled it! I was going back to our Writers Group.

A couple of weeks later, I was warmly welcomed by our leader and other group members. It felt so good to be hugged and encouraged. We were given handouts with helpful writing tips. To my surprise, in large print on the side of one of the handouts were the words, "Hone Your Craft." Wow! This was the third time I had heard or read these words in just a couple of weeks. I knew God was speaking to me.

No longer would I doubt God's call for me or compare my writing with others. He wanted me to finish this book. So, I will continue to hone my craft, and with God's help, we will finish this book.

And so will you.

A Writer's Prayer

FATHER GOD, I believe You have placed in me a desire to inspire people with my writings. I want to lead others to You and help others walk closer to You, so Your *agape* love is revealed to them.

Please help me conquer the struggles pulling at me, keeping me from achieving this goal. Discipline me to push forward and write daily because You did not give me a spirit of fear, but of power, love, and self-discipline. Help me form the words in an eloquence that reaches those You would have them reach. Speak through me, Lord.

Help me fulfill Your purpose and Your will. You are the Potter, and I submit as Your clay.

In Jesus' name, Amen.

Sherry Elliott

We Have the Light
Patti Jarrett

How many times have I heard/read/told myself, "Writing begets writing?" Why do I keep doing things I don't want to do and not doing things I know I should do? As Carl Sandburg said, "There is an eagle in me that wants to soar, and there is a hippopotamus in me that wants to wallow in the mud."

I look at my Bible, all the words written therein. I think of the Author, the Inspiration, Creator of all we see, all that has ever been, or ever will be. I don't want to present you with Patti's words; something hastily jotted down and considered, "Done." I want the Author and Finisher of my faith to speak to your hearts, because He is the Only One who can make a difference. And what's the point in writing if we aren't going to make a difference?

Each of us has a unique history of experiences, and we have them for a reason. We are who we are, for a reason. There is a God-given purpose for every detail of our lives.

What if you were to sit down and write a few words about every memory you have? Every person who has crossed your path? What if you scattered those thoughts across the table like pieces of a jigsaw puzzle? What would the resulting picture look like when you put it all together?

I believe each of our puzzles would be interspersed with shadow and light. What about the puzzles of those who don't know God, and those who have no hope? Would theirs be one of those impossible puzzles where every piece is the same dark shade?

There is much darkness in our world. It is evident in the current trend of books, movies, video games, and music. Can you imagine what that does to a person who feels hopeless? This is where we fit into their puzzles. We have the light of life, this treasure in earthen vessels.

We need to draw near to God, and tell of His goodness. He will light our lamp and lighten the darkness. So . . .

Arise, shine; for thy light is come, and the glory of Jehovah is risen upon thee. For, behold, darkness shall cover the earth, and gross darkness the peoples; but Jehovah will arise upon thee, and His glory shall be seen upon thee. And nations shall come to thy light, and kings to the brightness of thy rising. (Isaiah 60:1-3 ASV)

Remove the bushel covering your light, and WRITE!

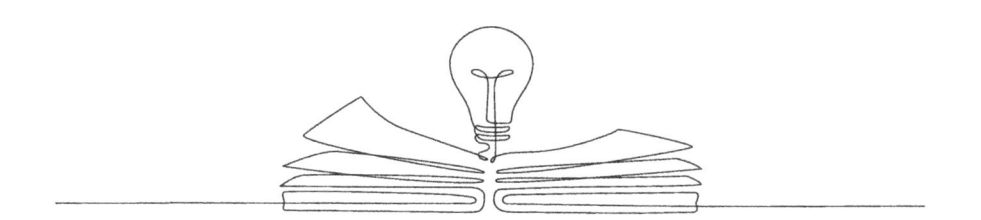

A Writer's Prayer

FATHER IN HEAVEN, You are the Creator of all things. In Your wisdom and grace, You granted us the gift of writing and the ability to create. While some create with a brush, writers use a pen. Through this gift of writing, You enable us to create stories, articles, and books that encourage our readers and evoke emotions from anticipation to zeal. Thank You for setting in our hearts a desire to communicate clearly and for giving us the ability to do so.

Help us, Father, not to neglect this precious gift! Let us be open to the leading of the Holy Spirit, so our work is truly inspired by You. Give us the desire to hone our gift so it can be used to its fullest potential. Enable us to prioritize so we make time to write. Help us overcome the obstacles and challenges that impact our writing. Use us, Father, as You see fit! Enable us to be efficient and effective. Help us to be true to Your Word that we might bring glory to You and be effective in the furtherance of Your Kingdom.

We pray in the Name of Jesus. Amen.

Joyce Kirby

More Than Technicians
Pam Piccolo

As Christians who write, we hone our craft with care and precision, taking pains to develop skills reflective of our gracious Creator. And so we should.

Colossians 3:23-24 admonishes,

Whatever you do, work at it with your whole being for the Lord and not for men, because you know that you will receive an inheritance from the Lord as your reward. It is the Lord Christ you are serving. (BSB)

Writing is skilled artistry to be sure. Even so, we're tasked to be more than technicians. Like Jesus' parable of building on sand, our literary houses of perfectly constructed sentences, airtight plots, and engaging personalities come to nothing eternally if not built on the firm foundation of faith in the wondrous God we serve.

The hallmark of a believing writer is that we create from a worship relationship. So, we give testimony to the One who loves us on His terms. We submit to His moral order, no matter how counter-cultural it gets. We bear witness to His restorative power, recognizing our own need for redemption. We acknowledge the miraculous, however inexplicable. We do all this behind the scenes, singing harmony to His unchanging melody.

Harmonizing has always been my bent. I'm a mild-mannered mimic, content to parrot the ideas of those far more inventive and insightful, albeit in my own particular voice and style. Over time, I've come to realize the value of being this kind of "recording secretary." It's an opportunity to bear witness not to "my personal truth" but to eternal TRUTH, a perspective lost to the popularized notion that faith and reason don't mix. There is indeed nothing new under the sun because God made it so! There's no shame in proclaiming this glorious reality that lies beyond the borders of our experience, no matter how often we repeat the theme. Perhaps in some small way, our calling is to do just that.

The Enlightenment of the 17th and 18th centuries began an age when reason-based knowledge enthroned the "almighty self" as the sole arbitrator of meaning and purpose. The majestic lion, once an obvious emblem of God's Kingship, was reduced to mere alpha predator equipped with violence to survive; the meek lamb, no longer the archetype of innocence, was seen simply as a tame food source for us "bipedal primates." This bombastic beat goes on with ever-expanding absurdity today.

As Christians, we know no such schism between imagination and reason, between supernatural meaning and reality, between story and science. What better reason to reclaim the conscious use of our God-given imaginations to produce works worthy of His eternal purpose and glory?

As Thomas Howard proposes in *Chance or the Dance? A Critique of Modern Secularism*, it's time we recover "the ancient glory of the narrative making the ordinary luminous."

Brett Lott in his book, *Letters and Life... On Being a Writer, on Being a Christian* drives it home:

"We as believers must see that there is no one save Satan who stills our fingers over a keyboard when we, with fear and trembling, begin to write of our 'human attestation' to the role of grace in our lives."

We are craftsmen, even artists, but only protégés of the Master. We are gifted, yes, but mere Salieri's to our Mozart. We are sojourners indeed, but still diplomats on a mission for a higher cause. Remembering these things is paramount. More than writers, we are Christians who write.

Questions for Guided Journaling

Do you see your writing as ministry? If so, what themes are most important to you?

_____
_____
_____
_____
_____
_____
_____
_____
_____
_____
_____
_____
_____
_____

Let each of you look out not only for his own interests, but also for the interests of others.
Philippians 2:4 (NKJV)

UNIQUE VOICE

And whatever you do, do it heartily, as to the Lord and not to men, knowing that from the Lord you will receive the reward of the inheritance; for you serve the Lord Christ.

Colossians 3:23-24 (NKJV)

"Close the door. Write with no one looking over your shoulder. Don't try to figure out what other people want to hear from you; figure out what you have to say. It's the one and only thing you have to offer."

Barbara Kingsolver

Writing Under the Influence
Jayne Ormerod

I know it's kind of like a magician revealing how his tricks work, but I am about to share with you the deepest, darkest secret of writers. I mean ALL writers. Anyone who has ever put pen to paper or fingers to keyboard or dreamed up a catchy little ditty in their head. But you must promise not to tell anyone because, well, then it wouldn't be a secret any more, right? Promise? Okay, here it is. Every writer across the ages and throughout the world has written under the influence!

Allow me to clarify.

I don't mean that writers are their most brilliant when under the influence of drugs or alcohol or even chocolate (although many writers I know do consider chocolate to be the universal summoner of muses). I mean every writer writes under the influence of someone whose words they have read, admired, and absorbed. Someone who inspired them with a particularly well-turned phrase, or brought them to tears with an emotionally packed passage, or sent their heart racing with a description so vivid it's as if the reader were teetering on a cliff overlooking an angry sea. An aspiring writer will read something so poignant or profound they whisper to themselves, *I want to write like that.*

It happens to all of us.

Agatha Christie admits that Conan Doyle had an influence on her desire to write mysteries. She credits *The Mystery of the Yellow Room* by Gaston Le Roux to having sparked the conversation between her and her sister about writing a detective novel.

John Steinbeck has undoubtedly influenced many, many writers, John Grisham among them. The clarity of writing made an impression on Mr. Grisham, and that style, when combined with his legal background . . . well, you know the rest of that story.

The Queen of Romance, Dame Barbara Cartland, gives props to Elinor Glyn. If you're not familiar with Mrs. Glyn's work, perhaps it's because you're too young. Her popularity peaked over one hundred years ago. While tame by today's standards, Mrs. Glyn's romances (and personal life) were considered scandalous.

Who has influenced that King of Southern Literature Pat Conroy? An easier question to answer is who *hasn't* influenced him. His 2010 book, *My Reading Life,* is an homage to all who have impacted his writing, from Shakespeare to Salinger. Conroy, in turn, has influenced hundreds, if not thousands, of writers himself.

The author who influenced me the most is Janet Evanovich. But who influenced her? She claims the two early influences on her work are Carl Barks (famed cartoonist who created Scrooge McDuck) and mystery writer Robert B. Parker. I'm not going to compare Janet's main character Stephanie Plum to Scrooge McDuck, but you can probably see a thread of comedic antics stitched between the two.

Every writer has been influenced, whether they admit to it or not. How do I know this? Because I believe the universal truth of what 19th-century clergyman and speaker Henry Ward Beecher had to say on the topic of life's influences:

"What a mother sings to a cradle goes all the way down to the coffin."

Wow. That's kind of profound, especially for those of you who may not have had your first cup of coffee today. I like it. Especially since the only other applicable quote I could find on influence was "Monkey see, monkey do!" (source unknown). No matter which way you say it, our writerly pursuits are impacted by the writers around us. What is "sung" to us does last us throughout our lives. Need proof? Raise your hand if you are still afraid of your cradle falling out of the treetops? See what I mean?

If you've ever read anything in your life (and since you are reading this I'm going to extrapolate and believe you have read millions, if not billions, of words), then you, too, are writing under the influence of a writer who has inspired you to dream, one who has shared your doubts, one who is a shining example of how determination can land you on the top of the Best-Of lists.

And remember, you promised not to tell anyone. This is our little secret.

Drowning Identity
Amy Heilman

I was treading water in the middle of the ocean with a man whose face I did not recognize. Our heads barely bobbed above large waves. Pieces of paper floated around me. I remember the feeling of fear and confusion.

One by one I recognized the floating pieces: my driver's license, social security card, and passport papers. Pieces of my identity. They were floating away, far out of my reach. The man held one paper that was torn and tattered and looked like my birth certificate. The man laughed, and I knew I had been deceived. I had been lured into deep, unknown waters, and he had stolen my identity. Before I knew it, this deceiver tried to pull me under the water.

I struggled to free my legs from his grasp and raise my head above the waves for breath. People I recognized casually swam by, waving and talking to one another. "Oh, she must be all right. She is with that man, so she must know him." I wanted to scream at them, but I couldn't.

What? Know him? He's been deceiving me! Help me! He's trying to drown me!

The deceiver continually pushed my head under the waves. Nearly choking on salty water, I lifted my blurry eyes to the sky, trying to catch a last breath.

Where is God? Doesn't He care that I'm drowning?

I awoke to my three-year-old son whimpering in the next room. The clock on the nightstand said 6:02 am, and I was out of breath.

That morning, still frazzled, I asked the Lord to reveal any significance of the dream. This was the first time I had ever asked this of Him. That day, in my Bible reading time, I came across Psalm 18:16-19 (NIV):

He reached down from on high and took hold of me; He drew me out of deep waters. He rescued me from my powerful enemy, from my foes, who were too strong for me. They confronted me in the day of my disaster, but the Lord was my support. He brought me out into a spacious place; He rescued me because He delighted in me.

This alarming dream was a pivotal turning point in my life. There was no longer a doubt in my mind that the enemy had been exposed.

I would no longer allow myself to be deceived. I started an intentional journey, choosing daily to allow God to renew my mind. With a humbled heart surrendered to my Creator, I determined to reclaim my identity as true image bearer of God.

Part of my true identity and calling is to be a writer and encourager through words. If the enemy had his way, he would silence me and drown out that part of me. However, our loving God knows how to get our attention. Through this dream, He awakened me to arise and take back my identity as His Beloved.

A Writer's Prayer

Good morning, Lord. I wake, my soul refreshed
Safe in Your arms.
All night my spirit soared, within a world
Created just for me.
My soul relaxed and carried to Your peace
While floating in the Words that are to be.

My eyes are clear.
My mind is set, to document what You did speak
To me deep in the night.

Hush, my soul.
Hear the words my spirit now records.

It's time to write.

Dr. James R. Boyd

Reluctant Writer
Julie Strohkorb

I absolutely hated adding the words "reluctant writer" to Jay's student record, but I could not have his fifth-grade teacher begin the year blindly. Perhaps she could coax him to produce the three paragraphs that I could not.

"I don't know what to say," he would explain blankly during our writing hour. I always responded to these "excuses" with praise for his keen understanding of Fortnite and Pokémon cards, cafeteria lunches, and foursquare. Surely, he had ideas worthy of a fourth-grade writing prompt. Despite my best efforts, though, I could not make Jay understand that his own opinions mattered.

What does a nine-year-old know? He knows his mother forgot to give him a sack lunch for the field trip. He knows he's the only kid in the fourth grade without a baby picture on the bulletin board for graduation. His soft-spoken suggestions are rarely taken by his peers. Jay has little evidence to believe his opinions matter.

In this sense, I clearly understood his struggle to craft a state-approved opinion essay with such prompts as, "Should one open gifts during one's birthday party or after the guests have left?"

"I don't know what to say," he complained again after another ten agonizing minutes on the clock. I mirrored his watery blue eyes, helpless to fill him in one afternoon with self-confidence.

How do I teach a child to realize that every anxious thought he defeats, even the victory of remembering his gym shoes, is word-worthy? Sentient moments are sacred. We all experience a mix of the mundane (when we nap) and the extraordinary (when God truly speaks.) A writer relates these points of clarity to others, or at least prompts a reader to understand we are not alone in a crowded lunchroom.

Oddly, I connected to Jay's bewilderment. His reluctance to write mirrored the way I found myself teaching fourth-grade writing, instead of actually writing. In an academic landscape filled with professional podcasters and PhDs, I truly felt I had nothing to say either. Years had gone by and I neglected to make even tiny deposits into a journal.

So, Jay, what is to become of us if we do not learn how to gather pitiful strength to practice speaking our minds? Be careful to give attention to your quiet thoughts, or you will continue the habit of swallowing them. Our experience is our experience. Our thoughts are our thoughts. God is speaking every day to us. He who has a #2 pencil, let him write!

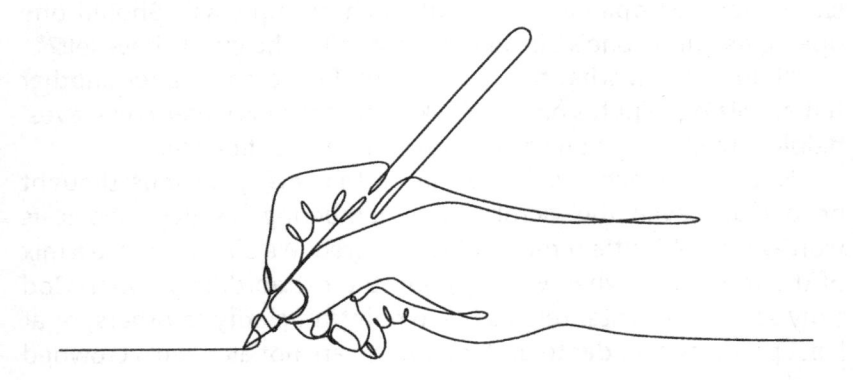

The Fabric of Life

Valerie Fay

During a message one Sunday morning, the pastor asked why we so quickly forget what God has done for us. We can we get an answer to prayer one moment, but "before the ink is dry on the page of our miracle," we succumb to "the habit of not living in what God has done and is doing."

Too often we retreat into despair or dread and the gloom of a world devoid of faith and hope. Instead, when things get hard, we must look back on the faithfulness of God. In that morning's message, the pastor said, "Get your past miracles out of the attic, and bring them back down where you live. Recall His goodness and give thanks."

Listening to his advice reminded me of a dream.

I found myself in the dark attic high above the old two-story house I was then living in. With the only light coming through a small window at one end of the room, I could see amidst the boxes and accumulated stored items a large, dusty chest, the kind made from wood with the top slightly curved. Iron hasps and leather straps held the lid closed. I was drawn to this and, upon opening my "treasure chest," I discovered all kinds of material, some of dark, solid colors and some intricately woven fabrics with jewel-colored threads. I lifted the pieces to examine each more closely, delighted with the beauty and variety of the contents. And then the dream ended.

If I close my eyes today, I can see the folded pieces of heavy material covering the more delicate fabric underneath. The image reminds me of the Old Testament tent of meeting. The place where the Ark of the Covenant, the focal point of the presence of God, was kept. The tent had four distinct coverings. The first and innermost covering was of pure linen on which figures of the symbolic cherubim were wrought with needlework in blue and purple and scarlet threads (Exodus 26:1-6; 36:8-13). Above this was a second covering of twelve curtains of black goat hair cloth (Exodus 26:7-11). The third covering was of rams' skins dyed red, and the fourth was of badgers' skins (Heb. *tahash*, a species of seal).

In 2 Peter, our physical body is spoken of as being a "tabernacle," an earthly dwelling that will one day be laid aside (2 Peter 1:13-14).

While in this world, the "fabric" of our lives will consist of many layers with differing colors. Each life will reveal a unique pattern. Some experiences are dark and others are light, like silk intricately wrought with thread woven by the hand of God. There are seasons now complete when God moved in our behalf; times when we knew not which way to go and a door suddenly opened before us. We have all probably experienced many answered prayers, unexpected blessings, and times of great trial when we were sustained through the storm.

Pick up again the past fabric of your life; admire the choice of color, the feel of the fabric. It was perfect to meet the need of the moment. Let our Lord stand beside you as you reach down to the place where past victories have been buried deep in your treasure chest, and thank God again for blessings long neglected.

Let's not forget that when looking at the underside of an unfinished piece of embroidery we cannot detect the final design; His work is not yet finished. We must trust the One who works all things together for our good and be thankful—for, *I am convinced and sure of this very thing, that He who began a good work in you will continue until the day of Jesus Christ.* (Philippians 1:6a AMPC)

Be Still and Know

I am in the hands of the One who knows me and loves me the most
Every intricate detail of my being, my life and current situation
Therefore, I have nothing to fear.

Be still, my beloved, the Great Gardener is pruning away
the unneeded dead branches
the unnecessary limbs.
Abide on the Vine.
This process is purposeful for the beautiful, best fruit
to produce bountiful fruit that lasts.

Be still, my beloved, for this fiery trial is burning off
the dross to create the purest, most precious gold—
Your faith, your whole being, consecrated unto God.

Be still, my beloved, on the Potter's wheel
is a masterpiece in the making
The hollow places made hallow by His hands.

Amy Heilman

Hearing the Voice
Dr. James R. Boyd

Writers are rightly concerned about voice. Our work must say something to readers, so it must have an effective voice to get the attention of those who are often overwhelmed with life. In a simple way, writers gather and process ideas to present dreams. With appropriate work, dreams can become reality. But, first, there must be a voice.

Your ears shall hear a word behind you, saying "This is the way, walk in it." Whenever you turn to the right hand or whenever you turn to the left. (Isaiah 30:21 NKJV). God's voice can direct and encourage.

Let me give you three H's that help us form our work and often give us a strong voice.

Hear—We must hear the movement of the world, the emotion expressed in the speech of others, and the changing of direction that happens frequently.

Heart—We must feel the beating of our heart as we experience life ourselves and witness the lives of others. This is where the true stories are birthed and told.

Hold—We must hold firmly onto the goals of our calling as verbal artists and to the desire to succeed on this road.

As Christian writers, we understand that the Word of God, in conjunction with the Holy Spirit, allows us to produce work that brings glory to God. We must learn to listen, knowing that the word we hear could reflect our experience, our desires, or our dreams.

We must be careful that we are not so focused on speaking (verbally) that we forget to hear the voices of experience, education, or edification. Scripture reveals that speaking without hearing is a weakness. Proverbs 18:13 states, *He that answers a matter before he hears it, it is folly and shame to him.* (NKJV) Listen to what your voices say to you before you speak to the world.

Writers answer questions of great importance through their words, such as those that relate to life, love, and future. If your writing provides enough answers to people who need them, they will listen to, and even search for your voice.

Your voice cannot be yours until you have activated your listening. Literary maturity requires living life, documenting what you have heard (lived), and then expressing your heart.

Hear the voice by speaking your voice. Hear the voice of others by reading their voice with empathy. Poetry encourages the practice of entering a solace of silence. Prayer closets are good for that.

In working through the process of writing, we are building ourselves. We know that our work will take a while to mature, and we patiently help it to improve. When the work is mature enough to launch out into the world, let it go. It will develop in time. There are other literary children who need your attention.

Hear the voice. It has guided you to this point. You cannot go wrong listening to it now. Consider that your work has an eternal impact.

When you pray, you are speaking to God.

When you read Scripture, God is speaking to you.

When you write, God is speaking to the world through you.

The Gift in the Voices
Sherry Elliott

Sam's pitch elevated, and his breathing raced. "Yes, I panicked. All the trauma from the past built up inside of me and before I knew it—"

Suddenly, there was silence. Seconds later, the silence turned to sobbing. "I didn't mean to hurt my brother. He was my best friend." As abruptly as Sam's voice entered my head, it disappeared.

I grabbed my cellphone to record the details in my Notes app. When I opened Sam's page, I saw notes dating back weeks to when I first heard his voice. He liked to talk while I washed dishes, so I nicknamed him Sam the Clean-up Man.

As I scrolled my notes, I saw a folder for other characters: Carol, Sara, Bob, and Dave. None of their stories were the same. Some voices were persistent, repeating the same story in my head day after day. I could be at work, focusing on my task, and Carol's voice would pop up, telling me the same story she had told me previously. She repeated the story to the point I wanted to scream, "Leave me alone!" That's when I recalled a writer telling me to write what I heard, and the voices would disappear. Good advice.

Now I have notes from these voices on scraps of paper, journals, on my cellphone, and on my laptop. Some characters introduced themselves to me years ago. Some have been around for decades. I've collected enough information to create first-draft stories, but then I stopped writing because of rules on grammar, editing, and "show, don't tell." Writing is difficult for me, so why would these voices choose me?

There've been times I've wondered if I was insane while carrying these random voices in my head. I was relieved to hear I wasn't alone. Could this be my assignment, my purpose? Could it be my mission to help these voices birth their stories of joy, pain, conviction, and love? What if I was a vessel God created to help others, but through characters' stories? Could my delay in putting pen to paper be a tragedy for the reader waiting to read a book that was never written?

"Just write," I hear them say. "Voice by voice, muse by muse. Create and don't delay."

It's been months since I've heard a voice. It's as if their job is done, and it's my turn to take all they shared with me to help someone else. Writing the story could bring a person comfort or a well-needed chuckle. It could teach the reader how to survive a traumatic situation, or how to love unconditionally. It could plant a seed, leading someone to inspire another person.

Millions of readers may read my book, or it could be for one person. That person may be in a future generation. I can see them blowing the dust off an old book in a beat-up box, in a dimly lit attic. That book may be the key to changing their life forever, all because of the gift the voices shared with me.

So, to all the writers with those voices in your head—respond to the gift. Fulfill your purpose and write!

A Writer's Prayer

FATHER, You have created a world full of beauty and wonder, filled with creatures of every variety and places of breathtaking splendor. You have made more people than we can imagine. Each is as unique as the next. Truly it is humbling just to observe the fraction of Your creation that I can witness. Not just all that is physical but the wonders within as well.

You have created us in Your image with spectacular creativity and amazing aptitudes. You have laid out beautiful and heart-wrenching lives for all of us, and You are with us every step. You know my heart. You know what is within it.

When I look out into the world and see the people around me, I am saddened to see so many faces turned down. So focused on a splinter that the beautiful forest around them goes unseen. I would like to yell and shout and scream, but I see the tools You have given me.

I pray that my pen will not just produce the observations of a simple man, but be a mirror. A way to reflect the beauty within us.

I pray that my words will not just provide some helpful insight into the world You have created for us, but be a magnifying glass. A way to show the beauty hidden around us.

I pray that my writing will not just be entertaining and informative, but be a hug. A reminder that everyone is a son and a daughter of the greatest Father.

In Jesus' name, Amen.

Benton Hammond

"Don't let the idea of perfection be the voice that chokes you."

Scott Wilcher

QUESTIONS FOR GUIDED JOURNALING

How do you combat the urge to compare yourself to other writers? Do you embrace the unique voice God has given you?

_____
_____
_____
_____
_____
_____
_____
_____
_____
_____
_____
_____

Do you have the gift of speaking? Then speak as though God Himself were speaking through you. Do you have the gift of helping others? Do it with all the strength and energy that God supplies. Then everything you do will bring glory to God through Jesus Christ. All glory and power to Him forever and ever! Amen.

1 Peter 4:11 (NLT)

STORY

Now to Him who is able to do exceedingly abundantly above all that we ask or think, according to the power that works in us, to Him be glory in the church by Christ Jesus to all generations, forever and ever. Amen.

Ephesians 3:20-21 (NKJV)

"My intent is to use story the way Christ used parables: to find something eternal that needs to be said, then wrap it up in enough entertainment so the reader will continue turning the pages as he or she is drawn closer to the heart of God."

Bill Myers

It Is Written
Kathy Daugherty

God said to Moses, "Climb higher up the mountain and wait there for me; I'll give you tablets of stone, the teachings and commandments that I've written to instruct them." (Exodus 24:12a MSG)

God, Creator of the heavens, the Earth, and all the solar systems, is a writer. More than that, He's a list-maker. As Creator, He could use any form of communication He desired. He chose writing. Granted, He chose clay tablets to begin with, and He used His finger, but He wrote. He knew some things were important enough that they needed to be inscribed—a way to remind us.

His first list (that I can find) is the Ten Commandments. These were details needed for instruction. For seven chapters, God talked and Moses listened. God gave instructions regarding blueprints, decorating, fashion design, law and legal processes, butchering procedures, woodworking, jewelry, and metalwork.

In Exodus 31:18, He finished speaking and gave Moses two tablets of testimony, sending him on his way back down the mountain. I'm glad it was Moses—his memory was much better than mine. I would have needed a much bigger notebook than two stone tablets. But then, He's God, and it worked for Him.

Think a moment—how many times does the Bible, one of its great prophets, or Jesus Himself, use the words, "It is written . . ."? There is a declaration in those words. The words that have been written have weight and purpose—a purpose of God.

What about our writing? Of course, it doesn't carry the weight the words of the Almighty do, but if we have been listening to that still, small voice, the words He gives us have purpose as well.

Have you considered the purposes of God in what you write? It is not just something we "enjoy doing." It is not simply a "hobby." It is a purpose of God that He has planted in us. Just as seeds that are planted don't all bloom at the same time, neither are our interests and callings all the same. Those same seeds, when they begin to sprout and grow, need care and cultivating. They don't just automatically grow into beautiful, sturdy, healthy plants.

He has given us the desire to write. It is for us to submit ourselves to Him for some of that same cultivating and care. He alone knows the plans He has for us. He alone does the "dictating" I hear in my ear when I sit down to write. They are not my thoughts. They are not my words. I am guided, I am directed, I am led.

Lord, may I tune my ear to hear You speak. For in Your hands, Your divine hands, it is I who am the tool with which You write. It is through me that others will hear those familiar words—"It is written."

The grass withers and the flowers fade, but the Word of our God stands forever.

Isaiah 40:8 (NLT)

Who Are You and Who Are You In Christ

DM Frech

Therefore, if anyone is in Christ, he is a new creation. The old has passed away; behold, the new has come. 2 Corinthians 5:17 (ESV)

Who are you? Who are you in Christ? Is there a difference?

Who are you?

Your talents probably come to mind, or quirks that describe you and only you. Choices you make, choices you don't make. You have characteristics unique to you. Even the way someone walks is unique to each person.

God made you so complex. No matter how old or young, there are still hidden parts you haven't even tapped into, a you, *you* still don't know. So, who are you?

Who are you in Christ serving God?

When God's Holy Spirit fills you up, when you pray, when you truly feel you're walking in God's will . . . *who* are you?

Between who you are and who you are when you're in God's will . . . that is, when Jesus is your guiding light, is there a difference? Some of you are thinking, of course, my spirit has been changed. Yes, maybe more than you realize.

I'll give some Biblical examples of people who were quite different when being who they were and being *who* they were serving God.

MOSES: On his own, he was painfully shy, tongue-tied. With God's hand on him, he became outspoken and led God's people.

DAVID: He struggled, committed adultery, murdered, and lied. But when serving God, God made him king of Israel. David wrote most of the psalms we read and sing today.

JONAH: God called him to preach to the people of Nineveh. His first reaction was to run. He was thrown into the sea, swallowed by a whale, and ended up in Nineveh as God's prophet. Why did God choose Jonah when he didn't want the job?

JACOB: He was dishonest, tricked his brother for a birthright, ran away from home, and wrestled with God, who changed his name to

Israel. For Jacob, who he was in God was about his offspring. Nations and kings would come from Jacob, including Joseph.

JOSEPH: One of Jacob's many sons, loved by his father, hated by his brothers who threw him into a dry well and sold him into slavery. Joseph ended up working for Pharaoh and saved God's people from famine.

In Christ, everything you think about yourself, everything you can do or can't do, is changed. Even if you think you know yourself, God sees you differently. In Jesus, you're not who you think you are. God has a plan for you. God thought you through and gave you certain traits for that reason, even traits you might not know now, a secret power.

Maybe, like Jacob, God sees who you are because of your children. Maybe God has already called you, but, like Jonah, you ran. Maybe you're in that whale.

God's will for you might be like Mary who had a physical calling. She gave birth to Jesus, and little is known about His childhood or how she raised Him. Though this calling was epic, we know little about her. God's assignment for you is designed especially for you. It could be for a moment Jesus has called you, or maybe, like Paul, God's plan is for you to be out there for the rest of your life.

Who are you? Who are you in Christ? And is there a difference?

Sure, God will use the talents He knows you have, but also God's purpose for you may be nothing like what you think you can do.

But in God's purpose you'll find a remarkable power of grace.

A Writer's Prayer

Father in Heaven, have Your way with this book I'm writing. I pray I can make the Bible clear to my readers, especially for those who find it difficult to read the Word and for those who haven't taken the time to read it.

I pray my readers will get a taste of the Bible and will want to read more of Your Word and want more of You.

May they discover You are real and alive and that You love them. I pray they will receive Your very life in them.

In Jesus' name, Amen.

Joyce Hammer

Lost in Translation
Pam Piccolo

In a multi-cultural world, it seems obvious that translation is a necessary aid to communication. But does it always lead to understanding?

What comes to mind is a classic episode of the Twilight Zone where we're introduced to the Kanamits, a race of 9-foot-tall aliens who land on earth with the expressed purpose of aiding humanity via shared technology. Trust builds as their advancements begin to alleviate world hunger, the energy crisis, and war. Expectations crescendo when a cryptographer's assistant decodes the title of a Kanamit book called, *To Serve Man*. Soon, earthlings are volunteering for trips to an alien planet described as paradise.

Only as the cryptographer boards the spaceship does his assistant cry out, "Mr. Chambers, don't get on that ship! The rest of the book *To Serve Man* . . . it's a cookbook!"

Exchanging the sense of words or text from one language to another doesn't automatically mean we preserve the intention of those words, language, or speaker. Getting to know the authors of that Kanamit cookbook could have saved Mr. Chambers from a terrible misunderstanding.

An illustration a little closer to home comes from one of my favorite books, *La Bella Lingua*, by Dianne Hales. From it I learned that to communicate in Italian, you must "see with Italian eyes, hear with Italian ears, speak with Italian rhythms." For example, double consonants should be held for three beats to avoid embarrassing slips like substituting the word for year with a crude expression for a body part.

Italians say that someone who acquires a language must "possess" it. So it is with the language of Scripture.

From the original Hebrew, Aramaic, and Greek, "the Bible has been translated into as many as 670 languages, the New Testament alone into **1,521** languages, and Bible portions or stories into **1,121** other languages." (Bible Translations—Wikipedia) How are we to become fluent in understanding enough to "possess" it—so that, much more than the exchange of information or ideas, we can grasp the truth and live it?

62

The apostle John gives us a clue when he writes, *But you have received the Holy Spirit, and He lives within you, in your hearts, so that you don't need anyone to teach you what is right. For He teaches you all things, and He is the Truth, and no liar; and so, just as He has said, you must live in Christ, never to depart from Him.* (1 John 2:27 TLB)

In *La Bella Lingua,* Hales quotes British author E.M. Forster who urges visitors to drop "that awful tourist idea that Italy's only a museum of antiquities and art." "Love and understand the Italians," he recommends, "for the people are more marvelous than the land." So it is with the Bible and its Author. Love and understand Him, and we'll be that much closer to possessing the language of Love.

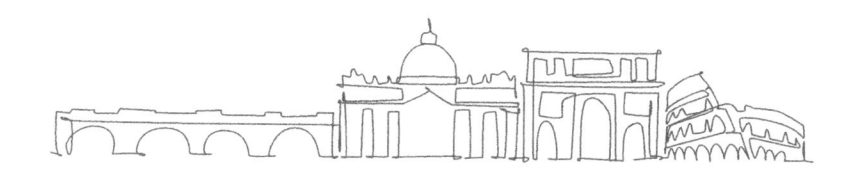

This Moment

Father, thank You for new beginnings.
The things we've done in the past are forgiven,
gone and already forgotten.
The past matters only in that it has
helped to make us the person we are today.
Your gift to us is life.
Our gift to You is
what we make of each and every day.
We have only this moment.
We may plan for a lifetime
but we have only this moment now,
to bring pleasure or pain,
to experience grief or joy,
to find fault and see only the things that are wrong,
or brighten someone's day with a smile,
and share love with those around us.
Lord, help me to see the world with Your eyes
and touch them with Your heart.

Kathy Daugherty

QUESTIONS FOR GUIDED JOURNALING

Regarding your writing, what priority do you give God's Word?

Instead, the law of the Lord gives them joy. They think about his law day and night.
Psalms 1:2 (NIRV)

UNIQUE MESSAGE

*Delight yourself in the LORD,
And He will give you the desires and
petitions of your heart.*

Psalm 37:4 (AMP)

"Fill your paper with the breathings of your heart."

WILLIAM WORDSWORTH

No Longer Self-Evident
Pam Piccolo

B eing Italian and raised in the north, I'm accustomed to loud and wordy communication. Imagine my delight in the fact that Christianity goes beyond a quiet, private faith to full-blown, word-based enthusiasm meant to be shared.

Just as our God spoke the world into existence, so He created and sustains our faith through His immutable Word. God's will is revealed in His Word. His truth is communicated through His Word. His promises are embedded there. Our Savior Himself is called the Word of God. It's how He's chosen to make Himself known. Psalm 138:2b drives the point home: *You have magnified Your Word above all Your Name.* (NKJV)

Because ours is a word-centered faith, we Christian writers serve God best when we write. Whether our writing encourages the faithful in what they already know or links the lost to God's purposes, we strive not to enhance nor alter Truth but to celebrate and communicate it. Sadly, we live in times when God's Word is no longer preeminent nor truths self-evident.

The Old Testament book of Judges describes such an age of moral chaos when relativism presides. It ends in this passage: *"In that day, Israel had no king; all the people did whatever seemed right in their own eyes."* (Judges 21:25 NLT) Surely, our generation can relate.

In essence, relativism rejects the objective reality of God and the concept of His divine law. Its tenets include:
- No universal, external standard for measuring truth;
- Thus, no applicable true/false, right/wrong, good/evil, beautiful/ugly;
- Truth is a matter of personal perspective. Preference reigns supreme.

Because we believe real meaning exists, we're accountable to understand and convey truth when we write. But how do we write for these times? How can we ensure that truth is central to our writing? How do we include Christian themes that penetrate the culture yet reflect the depth of our faith? These are challenging questions to be sure. I can only offer food for thought:

We can write with purpose, to edify, as service to the Lord and each other. We can choose clarity over cleverness, substance over rhetoric, using God's standard to measure truth without sacrificing cultural engagement or creativity. We can awaken imagination, leaving the efficacy of our efforts to the Lord.

Our minds were created by God to discover and embrace and be shaped by Truth. But with the fall, insight was darkened. Short of renewal, our thoughts become enslaved by our passions. The goal of language shifts from communicating to manipulating reality.

In Matthew 21:23-27, Jesus challenged the Pharisees to declare what they believed to be true about John's baptism. They hemmed and hawed and considered their options, not because the truth mattered but because their reputations were at stake. They then used clever words to cover their corruption.

Jesus responds to their dreadful display of mental gymnastics by dropping the subject. Tragically, His authority to speak truth was lost on them. Let's not follow their lead by shying away from telling the truth. Instead, let's stand on His authority and write.

Jesus Fire

Spread far your
embers ... 'til the whole
world remembers
the warmth in the
touch of His grace.
Build a fire of desire to
be empty of "me,"
To pull my "self" out,
cut it loose, set it free.
How sweet be the
hushing, of my cares at
the rushing of His love
into my new space.
Fan high the flame at
the sound of His name
'til we look on His
beautiful face!

Eileen Frost

The Word of Their Testimony

Derick Carstens

And they overcame him because of the blood of the Lamb and because of the word of their testimony, and they did not love their life even when faced with death. (Revelation 12:11 NASB95)

So faith comes from hearing, and hearing by the word of Christ. (Romans 10:17 NASB95)

Death and life are in the power of the tongue, And those who love it will eat its fruit. (Proverbs 18:21 NASB95)

As writers, we are given a tremendous amount of authority and power. Scripture says that the power of life and death are in the tongue. It further says those who venerate the power of the tongue will eat of its fruits. We have a great honor as wordsmiths to produce fruit that can nourish the soul and fill the belly of the starving.

Scripture says that man shall not live by bread but by every Word that proceeds from the mouth of God. Amazingly, we have the honor of penning nourishing words as the Father speaks them to our hearts. We have the ability to inspire hope or despair, build up or destroy, foster love or create hate. It's a powerful tool we wield. We may speak into someone's very heart.

As Christian writers, our glorious invitation includes giving language to the message that the Father of all creation is speaking! He's so personable and so creative that He has imbued each of us with our own voice, our own vernacular. He has given each of us a unique testimony by which we overcome the world.

We often get hung up in the lack of *grandioseness* of our story, so we don't pen it. We tell ourselves our story isn't impactful, it doesn't have power. We think, "No one will overcome by the words of my testimony." That's a dangerous fallacy. Even if your story was simply, "Jesus loved me, so I love Him," there is power to destroy darkness in that one sentence. There is room to expand that theme. I'm positive that there are countless stories of how Jesus loved you! Use your creativity to weave that testimony through your writing.

The final Scripture I'll leave you with is one of my favorites. Jesus said, *"By this all men will know you are my disciples; if you have love for one another."* John 13:35 (NASB95) The Father is inviting us to show His love through our words and our lives by simply loving. As writers, He is calling us to love our readers and reveal His powerful love! Remember this that even as Jesus poured His life out for us because of His love for us, so should we pour out our stories that others might read of His love for them and let faith grow in them that they might encounter Him and the richness of His love.

A Writer's Prayer

Heavenly Papa, You have put these passions and desires within me to be a writer. I hold them before You with open hands. Guide and lead my mind and my hands for Your will to be done and Your glory to be revealed.

My greatest desire is for the words on the pages to be an encouragement to the souls of others. To draw others closer in noticing Your presence with them and to help them grow in their personal relationships with you.

In Jesus' name, Amen.

Amy Heilman

Wherever He Leads

Sherry Elliott

My desire to become a writer started around the year 2000. I had read a "juicy" novel, but my only complaint was the cursing it contained. I wondered if there was a way to tell a juicy story without profanity. After giving it some thought, I decided to give it a try. To seal my decision, I wrote on a piece of paper, "I will become a bestselling author."

Almost twenty years later, I don't have a single publication of any kind. I think about that often, especially every new year when I look at the outgoing year and make resolutions for the new one. The last seven years, I've reflected on my desire to write a novel, and then I reflect on how many years have passed without my completing a single book. I feel like a failure. I have a stack of stories I've started but haven't completed. They appear to be a stack of thoughts that won't ever leave the bin under my bed.

How could this be? Well, characters pop into my head, telling me their story. They are persistent, so I jot the thoughts down. When I try to complete their stories, I'm reminded of the rules and guidelines of writing. The grammar rules, the story arc, antagonist versus protagonist, the beats, show don't tell, and on and on until I find myself saying, "Just forget it! I can't do this. It's too hard! Writing is not my gift. I'm out of my lane."

The negative thoughts go on and on, but for some reason, I wake up to a new day and decide to try again. One year, I decided to go back twenty years to the first characters that had popped into my head. I became determined to finish their story and publish it somehow, some way.

In 2020, I printed the first draft. I was so excited that day. It was an incomplete product full of grammar mistakes and random errors that first drafts normally contain, but draft one was complete. I was excited! Now it's two years later, and I'm still trying to improve it. Another new year approaches and still no completed novel, much less a bestselling book.

I've asked myself so many times, why don't I just forget it. Stop writing and disappointing myself. Stop going to writing workshops to learn how everyone else there is so much better than I. They know how to arrange every word perfectly on the page, and it comes to them effortlessly. It shows me how far I am from becoming the bestselling author I envisioned.

But something inside makes me pause from those negative thoughts. It reminds me I wanted to give Christians something to read without the profanity that is so typical today. I wanted to write for God's kingdom, for Christian readers who wanted to read a good juicy story without feeling the need to repent after reading the last page. I feel committed to get those stories out for Christian readers.

The fact I can't shake this feeling assures me that God doesn't want me to shake it either. He placed this desire inside of me for a reason. He knows my heart towards Him.

This year I've been thinking, maybe being a bestselling author is not the plan God has for me. Maybe I'm to be simply an author. Maybe, just maybe, I should have consulted with Him about the idea I had. Maybe I need to take a step back, consult with Him, and ask "Lord, what do You want me to do with these characters that pop into my mind?"

These thoughts made Psalms 23 so clear when I read verse 3b: *He leads me along the right paths for His name's sake* (CSB). This means God will lead me where He has for me to go, and they will be the right paths with the right purpose.

Where God leads me will be blessed, and it will be for His name's sake, which means He will get the glory. And ultimately that is what I always wanted—to draw all the attention to Him.

Thinking back, I am sure my goals to write were selfish. I wanted the glory and attention. I wanted my name to be recognized by the masses as a bestselling author. The person I am today has thrown in the towel on all self-centeredness. I desire for God to be glorified.

God loves His sheep, and His plan may be to use me to write one story or one poem that may speak to only one person. That one person is important to God and to me.

God is the one who knows the plans He has for me and all His children. They are plans to prosper me and not to harm me, plans to give me hope and a future. (Jeremiah 29:11)

I trust God, my Shepherd. And where He leads, I will follow. Join me and let's seek God's face and not His hand. Let's inquire about the road He desires us to follow. And, as He guides, let's put pen to paper, keystrokes to keyboards, and words to dictation. We can be the light our Heavenly Father has called us to be in our writing. Let's take the Father's hand, and follow Him down the path of poems, devotionals, short stories, novels, biographies, movies, and so much more.

Wherever He leads, let's follow.

A Writer's Prayer

HEAVENLY FATHER, thank You for Your Word that breathes on dry bones and gives them life. In my despair and my doubt, You hear me, You see me, You know me. You knit me together with the fabric of creation and love. You alone give me purpose, dignity, and worth.

Father, I pray You will use my words to draw others to You. Through my writing, may others learn to love Jesus the way You do. Please empower my weak scribblings and give meaning to my meanderings.

Jesus, in and through my writing, may You have the reward for the suffering You endured for us.

Holy Spirit, breathe life into each page.

In Jesus' name, Amen.

Derick Carstens

A Provocateur For Love
Steven Webber

As a child, I provoked my brothers to make them mad. But when I grew up, I decided to provoke others unto love and good works.

In college, I was a bit of a conniver. Each payday I would leave a small bouquet of flowers at the dormitory room door of one of the female students in our campus Christian fellowship. I made sure no one saw me. On the card, I wrote something corny like "We appreciate you." And always signed it, "Seulement Moi Heb.10:24," (French for 'Just me'). Months later, at a campus fellowship gathering, I sat next to Paul as another recounted returning to her room and discovering a bouquet. She had seen Paul leaving her dorm floor. So, naturally, he must be "Seulement Moi." I playfully smacked Paul on the knee for his kindness.

A couple of weeks later, I uncovered that Paul had also started delivering flowers anonymously. As the fellowship group was increasing, we joined forces. Although the cards had the same words and signature, we used our own handwriting. At one point, Paul made brownies, which we put in the mailboxes of all the campus fellowship men with notes of appreciation.

At the next meeting, as the group tried to figure out who had made the brownies, Paul and I sat there looking as puzzled as everyone else. Which woman had an empty brownie mix box in their trash? Having written the notes in my best penmanship, it was obviously a woman's writing. After several vain accusations, everyone agreed it was a great way to show appreciation to the men.

That Valentine's Day, Paul and I sent identical kids' Valentine cards to each of the women using the same wording but in different handwriting. As the intrigue thickened, it became challenging to keep a poker face.

Two weeks later, I received the call. Paul had been killed in an icy road auto accident.

As the group met to remember Paul, I honored him by disclosing that we were "Seulement Moi." Tearfully, I told everyone how much fun Paul and I had in provoking others in the group unto love and good works. My wreath had Hebrews 10:24 inscribed on it, *And let us consider one another to provoke unto love and to good works.* (KJV)

I thank Father for those few months of devious conspiring with Paul to provoke others in the campus fellowship group. Since we cannot keep secrets in Heaven, I suspect Paul has found other ways to provoke others. In time, this duo will be back together slinking around those golden streets.

That was my genesis as a Provocateur unto love and good works. Beyond flowers, I provoked others by listening or standing with them through tough times. For others, I would buy something they needed—a new PC, clothes for a job interview, car tires, or house repairs. Anonymity, when feasible, added spice.

Along the way, I stumbled upon another way to provoke others unto love and good works: training and encouraging others through writing.

Four decades ago, as the military academy students moved outside my ability to teach and encourage them "Mug-2-Mug," I started writing "The Encourager" and sending it to them. Each recipient was asked to renew their "subscription" annually. I was surprised by the responses and pursued developing my writing skills.

When composing, I often start with a question to focus the reader. Then I borrow a concrete example from the reader's experiences. That is my hook. Extracting details from that experience, I then parallel these known details with intangible parts of relationships. In doing this, I reduce unfamiliarity and unease with "new" truths that lead to change.

For example, for the medical professional, I may parallel the concrete experiences of patient interaction with interacting with one's spouse or children. Or use the long process of physical recovery to illustrate the months it may take another to learn a new habit.

After highlighting the parallels, I shape subversive questions to provoke contemplation of how that truth may interrupt their current relationships. My purpose is to provoke another towards experiencing the Lord Almighty as "Papa" and life-to-the-max as one of His intensely loved kids. And doing so requires leaving behind many of the former habits of life.

Using examples from the reader's library of experiences is not novel. One of the greatest storytellers, Jesus, used this technique to communicate many spiritual truths. As I endeavor to restore relationships, to "make it right," I attempt to mimic His technique.

Now in my patriarchal season of life, it is time to start compiling my stories. Perhaps in publishing, I will continue provoking others unto love and to good works.

Thus, Father, this is my request:

Give me insight into how common life experiences may parallel spiritual truths so that the reader will learn how to put off the old and put on Christ.

Give me wisdom to edit my experiences to blow away the smoke that may obscure Your transformational flames.

Untangle my journey of inner healing so that I may speak diagnostic words of hope and guidance to others. Use my words to stir courage in waiting on the Spirit, the greatest surgeon of the soul. Provide me discernment into the progress of one's healing so that I may encourage them to press forward. So many, in stumbling forward, do not perceive the progress they have made just by putting one foot in front of the other.

Remind me of my angst in taking risks on You. Whether sexual and relational desires, financial, or medical, You have created me to depend on You, to practice Your presence in the fog of the uncertain. Please do not let me forget this. And mold my story to encourage others to take similar risks when they are anxious, thereby experiencing a bit of Your life-to-the-max. Structure my message so that their confidence in You increases.

Father, I do hope that they will learn sooner than I did of what it means to practice Your presence instead of being a practical atheist most of the week.

In the name of Jesus, the One who opened the door for me to experience You.

City On A Hill

Every believer, every child of God
    is a candle lit by the
    ever-burning torch of Christ.

A light to lead others from
    their spiritual darkness to an
    illuminated relationship with Him.

Every believer, every child of God
    is a lighthouse,
    a city on a hill.

We cannot be hidden, but are seen
    from every direction.

Do we shine forth so that others
    can see the way to enter into God's Kingdom?

"You are the world's light, a city on a hill, glowing in the night for all to see." (Matthew 5:14 TLB)

Elizabeth S. Green

Everyday Miracles
Pam Piccolo

I recently ran across a fascinating documentary called *Patterns of Evidence—The Moses Controversy* by investigative filmmaker, Tim Mahoney. In it, Mahoney engages scholars in the fields of Archeology, Egyptology, Theology, and Linguistics to determine if the historic Moses could have written the Torah—the first five books of the Old Testament scriptures we call the Pentateuch.

Exodus 24:4a tells us, *And Moses wrote down all the words of the LORD.* (NASB) Did Moses have the ability to write eyewitness details of the Exodus journey, or is the Bible a collection of oral traditions passed down and recorded after the fact? Who wrote the Torah? When was it written? How important is a direct connection to Moses' authorship?

Working from a different paradigm, mainstream thinkers discount the Bible as history, distrusting it as an assortment of stories from multiple authors given to exaggeration and hidden agendas. Dating the Exodus during Egypt's New Kingdom period of 1250 BC, they doubt written Hebrew even existed at that time.

Ironically, by interviewing noteworthy—yet primarily disbelieving—experts, Mahoney follows the evidence to an earlier Exodus date of 1450 BC to conclude that Moses had access to a written language sufficient to have recorded Israelite history during the 40 years of wilderness wandering as instructed by God.

Searching for patterns that match biblical events with history, Mahoney looked for a written language similar in form to Hebrew that would have existed at the time of the Exodus and found a Proto-Sinaitic script that first appeared during a narrow 12-year window matching Joseph's time in Egypt. Despite the common bias in modern archaeology against the biblical record, this mystery script existed during Moses' time, looked like and was readable as Hebrew, and matched Israel's migration from Egypt to Canaan. As prince of Egypt, Moses would have had access to it.

Whoever invented this pre-Hebrew alphabet was a Semite, fluent in hieroglyphics, motivated to communicate with the masses, and living in or around Egypt. The first descendent of Abraham to arrive in Egypt was Joseph. As second only to Pharaoh, Joseph would have been required to read and write hieroglyphics, a system of some 1,000 distinct characters. To have distilled it into the precursor of Hebrew would have taken genius. Although a writing system of glyphs, the Hebrew alphabet in traditional form consists of only 22 consonants, a simplification difficult to explain.

To recap, the oldest alphabet with Hebrew connections existed at the time of the Exodus in the region of Egypt. The use of this simplified alphabet would have allowed Israelites to read, understand, and preserve Moses' words. Before the alphabet, only the elite had access to written knowledge. Moses' use of the alphabet made the written word accessible to all. Neither this basic technology, nor Moses' words, have been replaced in nearly 4,000 years.

What if the alphabet's invention didn't have a human source? The Bible itself proclaims divine inspiration (2 Timothy 3:16). Could it be that the alphabet's genius was a gift from God to a particular people at a particular time with the prime purpose of communicating God's Word to mankind, beginning at Mt. Sinai with the 10 Commandments?

Exodus 31:18 states, *When He finished speaking with Moses on Mount Sinai, He gave him the two tablets of the testimony, stone tablets inscribed by the finger of God.* (HCSB)

If the alphabet's arrival in history is no coincidence, but a gift to retain the knowledge of God, what does that mean to the writer? As compelling as fantastic miracles like the parting of the Red Sea are, everyday miracles like the alphabet abound. Every time we put pen to paper or tap on our keyboards, there's that same potential to make Him known. Whether through manuscript, poetry, journalism, even song—the possibilities are limited only by our availability and determination. Let's follow His lead and write!

Now to Him who is able to do immeasurably more than all we ask or imagine, according to His power that is at work within us, to Him be glory in the church and in Christ Jesus throughout all generations, for ever and ever! Amen. (Ephesians 3:20-21 NIV)

To Carry the Light

I'm going where highways are crooked and deep cracks can be seen
Where great danger is present and thick darkness deceives
Lies grab for the heart—and they blind each man's mind
I'll carry the Light, I'll stand on the height
I'll call to the lost, and I'll offer them sight.

The place where I'm going the sun doesn't shine
The fields are all barren, the trees are all bare
No moisture falls here, the ground's always dry
Dead leaves on the ground
And drab colors abound.

When I walk with my Lord, and His presence I sense
With a sword in my hand and a shield by my side,
His Truth I'll declare.
I'll trust in His Word, I'll run my race
And I'll not be afraid of the foe I might face.

Valerie Fay

Questions for Guided Journaling

What sets your soul on fire? How do you incorporate those passions in your writing?

_____
_____
_____
_____
_____
_____
_____
_____
_____
_____
_____
_____
_____
_____

They said to each other, "Did not our hearts burn within us while He talked to us on the road, while He opened to us the Scriptures?"
Luke 24:32 (ESV)

"Our doubts are traitors,
And make us lose the
good we oft might win
By fearing to attempt."

WILLIAM SHAKESPEARE

Photography by DM Frech

Part 2: Doubts

*The name of the LORD is
a strong tower;
The righteous run to it and are safe.*

Proverbs 18:10 (NKJV)

The Ministry of Listening

Evelyn J. Wagoner

I miss Helen Atwood. Whether you knew Helen or not doesn't matter. I hope you're blessed to know someone with her gift. Um . . . talent? Skill?

I should back up a bit.

I've been a bit angst-y lately. (Yes, I know that's not a word.) A bit discouraged. Wondering about this writing thing. About ever getting published. About ever getting someone to even look at my work. All that stuff that drives a writer a bit nuts. Now don't get me wrong, I know all the right answers. I know them because I'm constantly telling everyone else all those right answers. I know I just have to keep writing, keep pitching, keep putting myself out there. As we said in our first KPC Writers Group challenge: *Write what brings you joy, trusting God to use it for His glory.*

Easier said than done.

Sometimes the truth that's in your head has a hard time sinking into your heart. Discouragement soon follows. Am I really supposed to be doing this? Maybe I should just encourage other writers and let myself off easy. But the thought of giving up hurts like a meat hook lodged in my chest.

I, like others, often quote Thoreau incorrectly. "Most men lead lives of quiet desperation . . . and go to the grave with the song still in them." I'm confident that's not what I want for myself, a life of quiet desperation, going to the grave with my song still in me. (Though if you've ever heard me sing, you might prefer that I do.)

But back to Helen and one reason (there are many) I miss her.

Whenever this sweet woman asked how you were doing, she truly wanted to know. And for those moments when you had her attention, you felt as if you were the only person in her world. Whether she'd learned this or was gifted with the ability, she knew how to listen. Really listen.

I've needed someone like that lately.

Please don't get me wrong. I have an amazing husband and wonderful friends and family who will patiently listen. They all encourage me, and they truly mean the nice things they say. But it's hard bucketing out all that torment to those who are closest to you.

They worry. And they don't know what to do to help.

How does someone really listen? Tim Keller, in *The Freedom of Self-Forgetfulness,* says, "The thing we would remember from meeting a truly gospel-humble person is how much they seemed to be totally interested in us. Because the essence of gospel-humility is not thinking more of myself or thinking less of myself, it is thinking of myself less."

I think he wrote that about Helen. She knew how to do that.

Not long ago, I was having one of "those days." I met a writer friend for lunch. We talked about lots of things. Somewhere in the middle of it all, I cracked open a bit and squeaked out a little of my discouragement, then we went on to other things. I left, carrying my anguish with me. And missing Helen.

Later that afternoon, I received an email from my friend. She felt she had failed me as a sister-writer because she had rattled off a few words without waiting to listen long enough to see if that was what I truly needed to hear. Then she said, "So let's try this again. What I'd say to you, if we had more nachos (which I could totally go for right now) and more time together, is more like this." She wrote of hurting hearts and how life with a creative gift never gets easy. She reminded me of Elijah, who curled up under a juniper tree and wanted to die right after he had called down rain and outrun chariots. She reminded me of Moses who got his calling directly from God and still believed he couldn't do it.

Then she talked about the fire in our bones and how, no matter how we try to shut our mouths (or still our pens?), it will roar louder and louder. She talked about the panic and the terror. And the aches. Oh, the aches. How the ache of "waiting" is a worthy ache, but the ache that is NOT born of waiting-in-hope but from fear that I won't ever be satisfied, that I won't be whole, that I'll crave and suffer and long for *no reason at all*. Well, that's a devilish ache. It's the voice that tells you that you were crazy/foolish/wrong to ever think He'd choose you for this. That at this point the only thing to do is stick your writing desires in a suitcase under the bed. Go back to what is comfortable, what doesn't gnaw on your soul, what you know you can do easily and well. Go now and you could mitigate the damage.

There was more, all of it a balm to my soul.

I came away refreshed, recharged. Yes, a lot of that had to do with the fact that she was totally on the money. She started off apologizing, and yet it was so obvious that she had listened beyond my words, and she cared enough to give a thoughtful response overflowing from her heart.

I knew I had been heard. And it meant everything.

Is it a gift, a talent, a learned skill, or maybe a fruit? I can learn a lot from Helen Atwood and my sister-writer.

So, how are you today?

I'm listening.

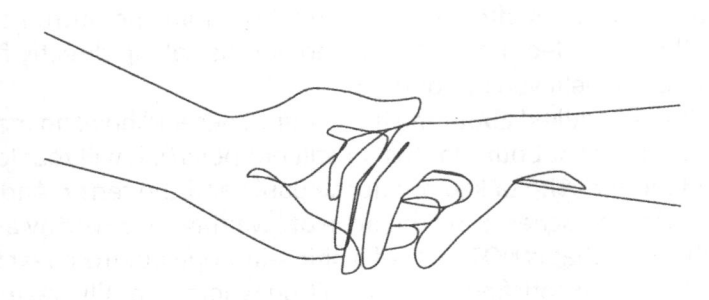

Confessions of a Fear-Based Writer
Yvonne Saxon

In a room full of faith-based writers, I know I'm the odd one out. I feel like I'm not supposed to be there. They'll find out I snuck in and show me to the door. Why? I'm an imposter.

While I sit and admire the writers of brilliant Bible studies, dazzling devotionals, faith-filled fantasies, and inspirational romances, I'm sinking in my chair. Who am I? I don't have anything to say like that. I write, well, regular stories. I'm afraid I'm not in the same league as everyone else in the room.

I do want to glorify God with redemptive themes and beautiful prose, but another fear echoes in my head: I'm not as good a writer as they are. Take writing prompts, for example. After a five-minute writing prompt, I'm listening to masterpieces being read while mine sounds like a first-grader trying to tell a joke . . . with no punch line!

And what about getting published and marketing and all that? My fear that no one will want to read what I've written is followed by the twin fear that maybe someone will—I can hear the laughter already. The doubts and fears go on and on.

So how do I go from a fear-based imposter to a faith-filled writer? Trust.

I've thought about engraving Psalm 56:3 on every pen, tablet, and laptop I use. It says, *When I am afraid, I put my trust in you.* (ESV)

Instead of asking, "Who am I to write this?" I ask myself, "What experiences have I had? What story is God telling in my life?"

When I don't feel my writing is as good as other writers, I'm tempted to dig a hole and bury my one "talent." Instead, I need to put it in a basket and present it to my Savior like loaves and fishes, trusting Him to increase it as He sees fit.

When the doubts and fears in my head become louder than a thunderstorm, I can quiet them by working hard, gathering resources, and remembering Colossians 3:23, *Whatever you do, work heartily as for the Lord and not for men.* (ESV)

I may still be a little odd, but I'm no longer the odd one out. I am supposed to be here, and unless I tell one of my corny jokes, I won't be shown the door!

Run to the Lion

He has come—
The Lion
has come
calling us to
His eternal tribe.
Fearful power—
that's His wonder.
All who hide
in His mane
will prosper.

Wee little children
simple in heart—
cling to Him,
believe without doubt,
depend on Him
for all they need—
They are who
He calls
His own.

Run to the Lion—
Hide in the strength.
Hear Him call
With a mighty,
loving purr.
Ask for protection,
He'll be
at your side.
He has come—
Run to the Lion.

Jessica Snook

Who I Am Meant to Be

Lori Higgins

Sometimes claiming I'm a writer is a struggle. There are days when I type away and fill up the once-blank pages with ease, but there are also days where that page stays empty. Or the words do appear, but then I hit that backspace key, never getting anywhere at all. Those are the times when I question who I am. Who I want to be.

I fell in love with stories as a little girl. As I grew, I told myself I would be a writer one day. Soon after, I started a handful of never-finished books and life became busy, as it is prone to do. The dream faded during that time. Then I had a resurgence that came from a place deep within.

I all but panicked the day I decided to begin writing the novel, the one that had churned in my mind for years and felt like it would burn me alive if I didn't get it down on paper. Doubts plagued me. I longed to tell a story in such a way that the reader would become so lost in it that words would no longer appear on paper. Wanting to be able to look back on my novel and know I had written to the best of my ability felt formidable.

It has been a few years since I made that decision, and I still struggle with those thoughts. Even on the days I feel accomplished and a little bit lighter having written what needed to be told, the feeling is still there lurking in the outskirts of my mind. On bad days when I struggle to focus and have a dozen distractions thrown at me, the voices are louder. The doubts creep in and I again question myself. Focusing on my task becomes a struggle, as my mind races with all the other things I should be doing with my time. I feel like I'm drowning. On some of those days, despair settles over me, and I must shake myself from it. My creativity feels like a damp fog has fallen, and my characters' loud voices become faint whispers. Yet, they still talk despite it all.

I must remind myself of who I am, of who God has created me to be. The good days are on the horizon and, when they come, I feel that amazing sensation of being utterly alive. Writing is like a healing balm and soothes my overworked nerves. The thoughts that would slow me down and tear me from the inside fade. My mind awakens with a flow of creativity, the most welcoming of sensations, and I write seamlessly until I no longer see the words as the story plays out before me.

On those days, distractions dim, and I'm lost in another time, in another life that is not my own. The words that threatened to leak out through my pores as they built up inside of me come, but, just as quickly as they do, they can also stop. Words will at times elude me, and I pause. My heart, still thrashing from the euphoria of writing so fast, is all I can focus on. I stall as the rest of the screen seems to grow brighter, and nothing comes from my fingertips. The blankness taunts me, and my mind screams at me to write something, anything. But my heart wants it to be great, worthy to be read.

In that moment, I must remind myself that writing is never wasted. Typing one word after the other, even if no one ever sees it, still makes it worthwhile. Even if I delete it all, my mind is giving itself practice. I don't have to write in elegant words and leave the reader breathless with my sense of grandeur. I just must share what I can. Writing is its own reward, and it's the reason I do what I must.

My favorite moments are when the characters in my story dictate what needs to be told, and I am nothing more than their scribe. Yet, those pesky worries still like to poke their heads out of the ground at my feet and plague me.

At my worst, I wonder if I am good enough. I have been haunted all my life by feelings of inadequacy. Worries that I am not good enough in most things I do. Those thoughts tend to worsen when it comes to things I love, like writing. Doubt shadows me and questions if I have the creative talents to keep my work interesting or enlightening enough to read. If the words I write will even be enough to hold anyone's attention long enough to read past page one.

Even as I write these words, I worry that I am not conveying my thoughts well. The temptation to hit the delete button is growing by the second. This is when I remind myself that writing is never wasted nor is the time poorly used. I can't let my younger self down. My once childhood dream has grown with me and is now my adult dream. My goal. I will not let the little girl down who used to dream up stories of times long past and characters who wished to be known. I long to make that little girl proud.

I desire to hold my finished work, to run my hands over my name in print knowing that its pages hold the deepest part of my mind and heart, and others will finally get a glimpse into the dimensions of myself no one has ever seen. It is exhilarating and intimate.

This fuels my need to write without fear and to be proud of what I share. I long to see my books in a brick-and-mortar store and to be able to sign my name for readers who love to read as much as I do. I will be happy if only one person reads what I write.

I know I am not alone in these struggles, and we must keep going. If you ever need to pause, to refresh your mind before you can resume, take that moment and be kind to yourself. Offer yourself grace. There is nothing wrong with rest. Your writing will wait for you. Characters mid-scene will wait to be directed on what to do next. Eat, sleep, and pray. For as wordy of a person as I am, my prayers tend to be simple. I rest in the peace that God knows my heart, and I can speak to Him like a child who is trying to understand her own thoughts.

A Writer's Prayer

Loving God
help me
to forget
the yesterdays
that
i might have failed
and
to live
expecting
Your success
Now
Amen!

Merle Mills

H-A-P-P-Y

Karen McSpadden

Lamentations 3:22-23 The steadfast love of the Lord never ceases; His mercies never come to an end. They are new every morning. Great is your faithfulness. (ESV)

It was the week of my birthday and the kind of boldly brilliant Tuesday morning that almost makes one forget aging, the brevity of youth, and impending death. At forty, it isn't the wrinkles and chin hairs that wear me down . . . it's mortality. It's being alive in a world of incredible beauty and wonder, yet knowing I'll only get to experience a thimble-full of it all, if I'm lucky. Just a cursory accounting of the sheer number of books I'll never read is almost enough to send me to bed, curling under the covers indefinitely.

But back to that beautiful Tuesday. I'd spent the morning at the piano, so by the time I pulled onto the interstate headed into Norfolk, I was music-drunk and singing merrily at the wheel. The Elizabeth River sparkled to the right. Sparkled. That's how sunny it was. I love our Atlantic Ocean, but the water of the Elizabeth, right by a certain stretch of the westbound 264 Interstate, is my favorite water in the world. It turns the most remarkable blue on a bright day. So, there I was, music and sun and sparkles and rivers, and it hit me:

I was happy.

Absolutely happy, in the feather-light, free-floating, life-loving way that I had not been for quite some time. I don't know how it happened, but there I was, immersed in this perfect moment.

H-a-p-p-y.

That thought was followed in about five seconds by another thought:

It's not going to last. This morning, this moment, this weightlessness of soul . . . it's just about as fleeting as the sun on that river. Your brain will return to its regularly scheduled raincloud soon enough. The anvil always drops. You've lived long enough to know this.

I admitted it was true. I knew it.

And, as if that wasn't enough, an even worse thought followed that one—

The next time you're solidly depressed, you won't even be able to remember what it felt like to be in this moment. You might remember the fact of it—maybe—but you won't even be able to imagine what this happiness is. Even your body will forget.

I had to admit that was true, too.

But then my optimistic side (despite being outmanned and outgunned) jumped into the fray with a helpful suggestion. *Maybe if you focus, if you really pay attention to what it feels like to be happy right at this second, then you will remember. Be intentional. Concentrate. Then the next time you're all dark-hearted and dismal, you can pull this morning out of your pocket like a warm stone. Lock this moment in! Keep hold of it!*

For about another five seconds I did just that.

Then I realized that if I stepped out of what I was experiencing to capture the moment, that'd be it. What happens when you grab at a soap bubble? Pop. Empty air and sticky hands. Yes, it will pop eventually, anyway, but if I just leave it be, shimmering and suspended, it will have its own time.

With a sudden shock of relief, I realized I didn't need to be afraid of the bubble bursting. I didn't need to grab at the happy moment, or inscribe it on my brain and body. Because even though it would fade, inevitably, and even though I would forget how it felt or perhaps even that it existed, someone else would not forget. God would know. Like a wise trail guide, He knows when my heart needs to stop and be amazed and when it's time to keep slogging through underbrush. Because He knows the trail—because He built the trail—He already knows where the next moment of pure joy is waiting for me. He knows where the next dark stretch is waiting, too, when I'll enter it, and when I'll leave. Shadow and sun. I don't have to scribble my own map to know that happiness will surprise my soul because God delights in His children. He delights in us in the dark, too, just so you'll know, but sometimes He knows it's time for us to be giddy and lighthearted. And He knows how to get us there.

I was effortlessly, effervescently happy, all that morning, and even into the rest of the day. It was lovely.

Later, I thought about this in terms of my writing, or rather, my not-writing. I've been doing a lot of *not-writing* lately. I'm quite good at it. I can do pages and pages of nothing every day, like a professional. But one of the things that makes it so hard for me to write something is that each moment of creative work comes with both relief and dread. Right now, It takes a lot for me to get into a writerly frame of mind. I have to hack my way through brambles and thorns and bracken just to get close. And . . . what if the next time, I can't do it? What if I forget the way? What if I forget even how it feels to create, to lose my anxiety and my self-consciousness in a steady, thrumming beat of joy and purpose? As soon as that writing energy starts humming, I start waiting for it to leave me again. Words sputter out. I go back to not-writing, which is easy and effortless but also deadening. Mortality, remember? Chin hairs? I don't have forever to do this work, and something in my heart *needs* to do it.

And God knows.

He knows where those Deep Writing moments are and how to get me there. He knows how to navigate the stretches in between, how to keep me on my feet. There'll be plenty of mornings when I sit down to write through sweat and toil. Plenty of mornings when I don't sit down at all because it takes every bit of my energy to wash the dishes and walk the dog and love my family. But, just like my day of surprise happiness, a morning will come when my ordinary labor of writing is swept up into a dance. Everything will be light. Everything will flow. I'll remember what I'm here to do. My writer's heart will shout and scream for joy like a kid on a merry-go-round.

It's coming. I'm waiting. I'm open wide.

When Doubt Creeps In
Penny Hutson

Isaiah 41:10 says, *Fear not, for I am with you; Be not dismayed, for I am your God. I will strengthen you, Yes, I will help you, I will uphold you with My righteous right hand.* (NKJV)

This scripture reminds us that we have nothing to be afraid of or worried about because God has our back. Yet, as writers, we are often filled with doubts and fears. We question if our work is good enough. If we're working on the right project. Are people being honest when they say they like our work or are they just being nice? We worry we'll get bad reviews, or our book won't sell.

Sometimes we're more afraid of success than failure. If we get a book contract, we're on the hook. Now, we *have* to write. What if we lose interest or get writer's block or can't meet the publisher's deadline? Will we have time for our friends and family, or will our editors now consume our time? What if they ask for a second book we don't want to write?

As Christian writers we add even more doubts and fears to the mix. Will God like what we wrote? Will our Christian values come through in our writing, or will it be too preachy? Is this the type of writing God wants us to do? On and on we go.

In her now classic book, *The Artist's Way: A Spiritual Path to Higher Creativity,* Julia Cameron says, "Fear is what blocks an artist." And she says the ". . . cure is love."

Therefore, if we love God and believe He loves us, then there really is nothing to fear. The scripture tells us not to fear because God will help us. And not because of who we are but because of who God is. God's love for us is not thwarted by anything we can do. The Scripture even tells us how He will help. He will give us strength and "uphold" us with His "righteous right hand."

According to the *Merriam-Webster Dictionary* 1997 edition, "uphold" means "to give support to" and "to support against an opponent," as well as "to keep elevated." That's what God is doing for us when we're writing. When we get stuck, receive bad reviews, or are just feeling discouraged, He lifts us up and keeps us elevated above the fray, the worry, the concerns of everyday life, so we can write.

According to the Quest Study Bible NIV, righteousness is when "God brings believers into a right relation with Him." So, when God lifts us with His "righteous right hand," it means He is righting us, bringing us closer to Him, showing us, and giving us whatever we need to be in right relationship with Him. And that's important because when we're in right relationship with God, we're set. He's going to give us everything we need. However, if we're filled with fear, we can't follow the leading of the Holy Spirit within us or hear that "still small voice" of God which always directs us and shows us the best way.

Of course, we all know that fear and doubt are natural human instincts. We won't ever get rid of them or never feel them again. That's not the goal, but we don't have to hang on to those emotions or believe them. And we don't have to let them consume us. Acknowledge the feeling of fear or doubt, and let it pass. Let it go and turn to God.

With God at our side, we can do anything.

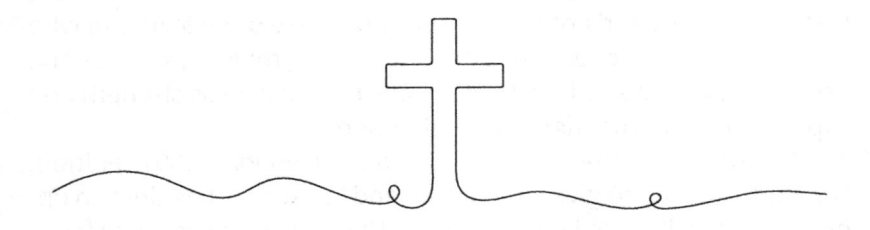

The Battle Within
Lori Higgins

I have been struggling with pesky thoughts and the feelings they bring. These thoughts settle lightly at first, but become heavier the longer they stay. Out of the medley of thoughts, two stand out. Sometimes they feel like beings from an unknown world, and in turn, I have named them Melancholy and Doubt. They are like soul mates, never apart. One never calls on me without the other. It didn't take long for me to find out that if I dare entertain them long enough, they will walk through my front door like a pair of old acquaintances who have come to visit. Their dark intentions at first seem unusually friendly. However, if I let my guard down and dine with them, without warning and much like leeches, they will sink their fangs into my tender flesh. They will drain me of any confidence I've ever possessed, leaving me empty.

It has taken me years to learn how to drive them away. To get rid of them, I must first acknowledge they exist. If you dare ignore them, they will hover like a damp shadow, and, before you realize what's happening, it's too late. They seep through the slit beneath your door, and cling to you until your feet draw heavy and growing despair begins to spiral within. They will demand to sit with you, and the cycle begins.

You can't let this happen.

The key to vanquishing them is facing them. Eye them through the peephole of your door. Acknowledge they are there. Then square your shoulders and throw a glass of your finest determination in their direction, and insist they leave. Only then will they turn tail and run. For a while, anyway.

Tonight, they are trying to visit me, and I want this to be the last time. I must bring myself to truly let them go. "No more revisits," I whisper, trying to keep my voice steady as my chest feels like it's cracking. It's odd how there is an almost twisted comfort in having them around. I first met them when I was a child playing outside. They took me by the hand, and I thought they were my friends. Their whispered lies soon proved otherwise. They have visited me since then, especially when I've felt my world brighten with joy and my confidence bloom.

It's almost comforting how I have come to expect them. Like ill-willed "friends," they are constant. Perhaps it's because they help me feel less alone in my thoughts. Sometimes part of me believes what they have to say. However, not too long after their visit begins, a little voice within tells me different. This voice grows firmer and louder until it's all I can hear. The truth fills my mind. I am more than what Melancholy claims of me. I am flawed, yes, but I am a soul saved by grace. I am meant for something important and worthwhile, regardless of how much Doubt wishes to claim otherwise.

Now, I feel them coming again. Like the cold mist on a rolling wave, the storm clouds are brewing. I stand as tall as I am able. I pray quietly for help, and somewhere deep inside I feel a warmth wash over my skin. Slowly it fans, drowning the icy needles of dread threatening to stab my heart. I gaze through my door's peephole, and the shrouded figures stare, their arms extended as though wishing for an embrace. An entry, anything at all. I inhale and allow the warmth to touch a sacred place they have never been able to reach—my God-given gifts, talents, faith, and soul. These are the parts of me they seek to cast a shadow on, but, being unable to, they simply lie to me. They want me to believe them, but I will not. Melancholy and Doubt cast their open-mouthed smiles at me. With empty eyes they beckon to come in and stay awhile, but I stand my ground.

No.

It's not a shout or even a spoken word. The word drifts in my exhale and hangs between us. This is all I need to do; I think so anyway. I hope. For now, they vanish, here one moment, and gone the next. However, if I am proven unsuccessful and they try to one day return like an unwanted vapor on the wind, I will keep myself plastered against my door and repeat these steps once more. No matter how hard they knock, I will not let them in. They can hover in their misery until they vanish again, because when it comes to vapors, there is a promise: Vapors fade.

Creative Beauty

i pray
that
nothing
will ever over-
shadow
the creative beauty
our Loving God
has placed
in the
depth of your soul.
Amen!

Merle Mills

Is Anybody Out There?

Merle Mills

Since I was a young girl, I have loved writing and have been writing seriously for the past 15 years. During this time, despite being a five-time book publisher, a contributing published writer, and a blogger with a worldwide audience, I often feel inadequate, because very few have responded or commented to acknowledge any benefit from my writing.

If you have experienced this same situation, I encourage you to continue writing and submitting to any platform that will accept it. I admit I have read but not responded or commented to authors/writers who have helped me greatly, and they may never know how much.

Keep on writing even though you too may never know whose life you impact through the gift of writing our God has placed within you.

Go Ahead and Quit!
John Reddel

"What would I offer a writer who is struggling?" John asked himself. "What would I say to me, a writer who thinks about giving up?"

"I think you should just quit," came a gravelly voice from behind him.

"Wait, what?" John spun around. There was nobody there. Strange.

"No seriously, just quit trying to be a writer."

John's head swiveled to the source of the sound—an older man sitting in a chair, paging through a newspaper. He wore a plaid shirt, khakis, and black rimmed glasses.

"It's too hard," the man said. "And who knows if you are even any good at it? Something would've sold by now, right?" The man raised the newspaper and peered over the edge at John. "The name is Stephen, by the way," he said, and then returned to his reading.

"You were just behind me." John gestured to the first place he'd heard Stephen speak. "And now you're over here." John pointed to Stephen. "How did do you do that?"

"Easy. I'm your imagination, so to speak. Your inner critic, if you will." Stephen lowered the newspaper and smiled.

"Where did you get a newspaper? Who reads newspapers these days?" John asked.

"Remember, you're the one writing this," Stephen said. "And it's starting to lag a little." He returned his attention to his printed pages.

"Right." John scooted toward Stephen. "So, why shouldn't I quit trying to be a writer?"

"You've got it all wrong. I think you *should* quit. Not worth the effort. It's too hard," Stephen said from behind the wall of newsprint.

"So, you agree with me? But you're supposed to be my critic?"

"It's a waste of time, not worth it." He put down his paper and studied John.

"But I do like writing sometimes, coming up with ideas, seeing where they go," John offered.

Stephen stood and put his finger to his chin. "Hmm."

"What's hmm?"

"Just hmm. I hear that you like writing, but not writing."

"It can be hard."

"Anything worth achieving is hard. I've heard it said writers don't like writing, but they do like having written."

"I do like having something written." John stood as he came to his revelation. "I do like writing. Hmm." He looked at Stephen.

"More hmm, but what about never being published?"

"So many rejections." John slumped into the chair.

"Your hero Walt Disney had many rejections and obstacles. He even lost his most famous character. Then he created Mickey. Imagine if he'd given up or quit."

"We'd be going to StephenLand."

"I do like the sound of that," Stephen said.

"I won't quit. I'll enjoy the process and see where it leads."

"Sounds reasonable." Stephen picked up the newspaper. "I thought a little reverse psychology would help you see the light."

John paused and then returned to the computer. "My inner writing critic-slash-psychologist? Who knew?"

"Let me know when you want to quit again."

"Will do." John continued pounding on the keyboard, then stopped and looked over to where Stephen had been sitting. "Thank you."

"The difference between winning and losing
is most often not quitting."
Walt Disney

When doubts arise, how do you overcome and get back on track?

But let him ask in faith, with no doubting, for the one who doubts is like a wave of the sea that is driven and tossed by the wind.
James 1:6 (ESV)

"Take a deep breath and tell us your deepest, darkest secrets, so we can wipe our brow and know we're not alone. Write like you have a message from the King."

ALAN WILSON WATTS

VULNERABILITY

*My heart is overflowing with a good theme;
I recite my composition concerning the King;
My tongue is the pen of a ready writer.*

Psalm 45:1 (NKJV)

God's Heart
Rachel Plumley

Each new year in writers group we are encouraged to choose a focus word to inspire our writing. One year my focus phrase was *God's Heart.* I want to discern God's heart for my reader! My prayer is that my readers will gain a deep awareness of God's heart through my work. God's heart is love! *While we were yet sinners, Christ died for us.* Romans 5:8b (ESV)

On the road to discovering God's heart for my readers, I must be aware of God's personal, passionate, present love for me. Friends, God wants us as authors to feel His love, which meets us uniquely to overcome each of our challenges.

God's love frees me from guilt!
Often, I feel guilty I haven't finished the project God placed on my heart. His love energizes me as a writer and as His beloved Bride. I am loved regardless of performance. When I let go of guilt, I learn that God's heart for my reader is for their freedom and joy.

There is therefore now no condemnation for those who are in Christ Jesus. For the law of the Spirit of life has set you free in Christ Jesus from the law of sin and death. (Romans 8:1-2 ESV)

Any barrier I face in completing my writing projects is no match for the powerful love of God. I may feel anxiety, encounter writer's block, or face schedule challenges. Sickness, tiredness, and shame can be healed with God's love.

Who shall separate us from the love of Christ? Shall tribulation, or distress, or persecution, or famine, or nakedness, or danger, or sword? . . . No, in all these things we are more than conquerors through Him who loved us. For I am sure that neither death nor life, nor angels nor rulers, nor things present nor things to come, nor powers, nor height nor depth, nor anything else in all creation, will be able to separate us from the love of God in Christ Jesus our Lord. (Romans 8:35, 37-39 ESV)

God's love frees me from shame!
Pride stops my progress when recounting shameful moments in my memoir. This is a process, but God is building my awareness of His love and eternal acceptance.

Be diligent to present yourself approved to God as a worker who does not need to be ashamed, accurately handling the word of truth. (2 Timothy 2:15 NASB)

The Word of truth frees us from shame and the lie that we're too sinful to be worthy of love.

Looking to Jesus, the founder and perfecter of our faith, who for the joy that was set before Him endured the cross, despising the shame . . . (Hebrews 12:2 ESV)

Freed from shame, I learn that God's heart for my reader is for them to be transformed by truth. No story is too shameful for God's redemption.

I experience His love and nearness through His Word!

Words are my love language. (*God Speaks Your Love Language* by Gary Chapman.) The loneliness of writing in solitude is overcome by God's love. God's Word is LIFE!

It is the Spirit who gives life . . . The words that I have spoken to you are spirit and life. (John 6:36 ESV)

That which was from the beginning . . . concerning the word of life . . . we are writing these things so that our joy may be complete. (1 John 1:1-4 ESV)

God's heart is that my readers will feel His nearness through His Word. I include Scripture in my work, knowing His Word is living and active.

How do I learn God's heart for my reader? By developing spiritual disciplines, I listen for God's voice before writing. My personal practice includes listening to God's Word on my new-favorite app: *The Courage for Life Bible*. I worship with full focus on Jesus, then keep a worship playlist running while I work. The Lord's Prayer is fueling my fire! Before I begin, it helps to call on my loving Father, asking for His kingdom to come on earth. O, may my writing reveal the heart of God for the beloved people of His eternal kingdom!

Ode to the Artist

The hands of an Artist
Gliding, molding,
pulling the shadows along
to the rhythm
of a waltz, a rhumba,
or any music
that dances in his mind.
Lovingly smoothing the clay,
passionately sweeping with the brush,
intimately etching
each detail
into design.

Each stroke is symbolic:
touching and reliving
emotions,
bringing to visual life
a character
found deep
within the person,
and normally experienced
by just a few.

Through his works
the Artist is opened
to all. All
see his hurts,
feel his fears,
know his desires and his joys,
simply by following the
movement behind
a stroke of his hand.

To all who
Experience
the Artist's
Power,
his hands are
Alive
with Fire,
and his creations come
as Gifts
from God
Himself.

Jessica Snook

Echoes of Eternity
Lori Higgins

Everything we know began with an uttered breath causing a resounding echo that reached every corner that could be reached. Simple phrases were newly spoken, and life began to stir. Then, somewhere within this span of existence, we were born and among the chosen.

We were meant to tell stories and share our thoughts. No matter how epic a tale you can weave or as short a sentence you can write, you were meant to be here. You were meant to write.

The call to write can be a heavy one. It can come with fulfilment, but also uncertainty. Sometimes it can feel almost too intimate. A glimpse into your mind on paper, a baring of your soul to a stranger can leave you vulnerable. Yet, never forget you were meant to write.

The idea never ceases to amaze me that we can dream up stories complete with a setting, dialogue, characters that all stem from our minds. A level of such complex creativity is certainly a gift. It only makes sense that such abilities come from the One who breathed life into us. We are His characters. He directs us. He holds us in the palm of His hand, and He loves us more than we could ever put into words.

He has given every soul on this earth talents, and it's our duty not just to preserve them, but to encourage them to flourish. Write the words that burn within. Write the words that you struggle to get out. Stare at the blank page and write despite it.

As writers, we can all hope our words will survive us, and we will leave a lasting impression on the lives to come. However, even if we don't, and our words become dust, they were once written and spoken. They matter, because we matter. Our lives will leave an echo. It may not be loud, but it will rest on the wind that will one day swell for the the writers that come after us, and maybe, just maybe, our words will echo along with those who came before us.

Please help me cause the echoes. Write. May your echoes join mine and become a song that rides the wind.

A Writer's Prayer

DEAR JESUS, You are the Author of my story.
You are my vision, my clarity, and my dreams fulfilled!
You are faithful to complete the good work You began in me.

Be my fire, my passion, my breath of life.
O Eternal One beyond time, I submit my finite time to You.
By Your grace, I commit to writing when You call.

Wake my spirit with Your song! In vivid style, inspire joyful poetry through my pen. Before I work, may I seek You daily. *In Your Presence is fullness of joy!* (Psalm 16:11)

Before I strive, may I rest in You.
May my writing flow from perfect peace and contented rest in You. May my readers see Your glory in my story.

In Jesus' name, Amen.

Rachel Plumley

Me Over Here, You Over There
Benton Hammond

Words are a funny thing. A little scary too. From our first moments on this Earth, we have something to communicate. Pain, hunger, fear, joy. Basic emotions that we can't help but express in some way. First thing most newborns do is open up and let out a hearty cry. In that cry, many things are communicated. But the most important thing parents are listening for is a simple message. I am here and I am alive.

I don't have memories of my earliest cries. I don't think most people can remember the first time they tested out their lungs. My first memory is the cry of my baby sister. She was but a couple months old, and I was approaching my third year on this Earth. I didn't know much of anything, but I heard her cry, and I understood that she needed some comfort.

That is a natural progression of a human. The first feelings are simple. The first thoughts even simpler. But, as time passes, the inner life of each human being becomes deeper and deeper. It isn't just "I am hungry." It is "I am hungry for something sweet." And then it is "I am hungry for the birthday cake I see on the counter over there." And eventually it becomes "I am hankering for a cake pop from Starbucks. Let's hit the drive-thru on the way home."

Early on, we can scream and yell and someone will decode the message. (Or at least keep trying things until the baby subsides.) And then we gain control of our limbs, and pointing and grasping becomes part of the arsenal. But it isn't very long before we need real communication. Grunts and vocalizations can't cut it forever.

My grandmother lived halfway across the globe when I was born. She didn't speak English, but she came over to spend six months with me. I didn't speak any language at the time, so we got along famously. A little *Sesame Street*, a little *Arthur*, together we started on the journey. We could describe what color her pajamas were. We could ask my mom to make another fantastic pound cake. We could say, "I love you."

Words provide a means to communicate the raw feelings and emotions and thoughts that lurk within all of us. Those basic feelings of pain, hunger, fear, and joy can be expressed through more than a single cry, and there is a whole host of more emotions to work out. Words could then take these emotions and form a bridge to transfer them to another person.

Here is where the inherent humor of words comes into play. A toddler will say and repeat any word or phrase in any order without knowing what they are saying. A younger child may understand the literal definitions of a word but not understand the context. A preteen may understand the context and not understand the gravity. A teen may think they understand the gravity of a word and not understand the consequence. An adult may get the consequence but not the personalized nuance and history the listener has. The many facets of a single word can go far beyond what even the most skilled wordsmith can handle.

Just a few days ago, I was chatting with some co-workers, trying to convince one of them that *The Wizard of Oz* was a book before it was a movie. We had a communication breakdown—a polite way of saying we had an argument. Round and round, we went for a couple of hours. Tempers flared, then cooled, then flared again. How could this guy not get what I was saying? I repeated myself until I could repeat my point in my sleep. Driving home later, I realized what I was missing. I was trying to communicate one idea, and so I chose the best word I knew. That word had a different definition and interpretation for my coworker. Words playing tricks on me.

Despite my knowing the definition, context, gravity, consequence, et cetera, of the word, I was fundamentally trying to portray a different idea to him than the one he received. It is incredibly easy to use the same word and mean different things. Sometimes even a slight difference can make a conversation go sour. And that is just looking at what is said out loud. The written word doesn't have body language and inflections to give additional hints.

That is my greatest fear when writing. Would that paragraph hit harder if I said what the misunderstood word was? Would the message be received in a happier voice if I wrote with more exclamation marks? Should I use bigger words so the reader knows I have read a thesaurus? Some words are copacetic in the moment, but what if they are totally unknown to a reader a decade out? Should I write in a stream of consciousness to bring the reader more into my headspace? Or is that alienating? The questions never end and the fear never goes away. Will my words ever be a real bridge between me and you?

I have an example of a best-selling book that continually has new interpretations. The Bible has about forty authors who wrote over the span of roughly two-thousand years. If there has been a book more misunderstood and purposefully twisted, I haven't heard of it. Every day, some verse is plucked at random and used for any number of purposes. And yet, people are still saved each day. Learning and growing and receiving. The Way, the Truth, and the Life. The Word. That is the key.

If the Bible, despite all the years, languages, culture shifts, and redefinitions, is still changing the world, why am I sitting here worrying about the opening word choice in a simple story? Ultimately, it is all in God's hands. Just write.

Brisk and Sunny

Seek and ye shall find
the good, the bad, the ugly
help in time of need
God wants you
to need Him,
to need worthy,
kind, ethereal
fountains of pure light
our glorious God
reaches with mercy
shines to embrace,
care for every step
your journey
brisk and sunny with
downtrodden gnomes
seeking repair
of fallen hope
wallowing
in ardent waste
coats forgiveness
with merciful grace.

DM Frech

"We are cups, constantly and quietly being filled. The trick is knowing how to tip ourselves over and let the beautiful stuff out."

Ray Bradbury

Questions for Guided Journaling

Are you willing to be vulnerable in your writing so you can connect to your readers? Do you find this easy or difficult? Why?

> But he said to me, "My grace is sufficient for you, for my power is made perfect in weakness."
> Therefore I will boast all the more gladly of my weaknesses, so that the power of Christ may rest upon me.
> 2 Corinthians 12:9 (ESV)

HEALING

The LORD is my strength and my shield;
My heart trusted in Him, and I am helped;
Therefore my heart greatly rejoices,
And with my song I will praise Him.

Psalm 28:7 (NKJV)

"It's important that we share our experiences with other people. Your story will heal you and your story will heal somebody else. When you tell your story, you free yourself and give other people permission to acknowledge their own story."

Iyanla Vanzant

Photography by DM Frech

Living in a Dream—Waking Up to Reality

Valerie Fay

The following is a chapter in the story of my life that happened nearly thirty years ago. It began in the springtime with a verse from the book of the prophet Jeremiah.

Gather up your bundle from the ground, you who live under siege! For thus says the Lord, "Behold, I am slinging out the inhabitants of the land at this time, and I will bring distress on them, that they may feel it." Jeremiah 10:17-18 (ESV)

I understood that Jeremiah was speaking to a people who were about to be invaded by the Babylonians, but I felt there was something more for me, and the Lord was telling me to hold on to these words. I remember sharing these verses and asking for insight from others, but the Lord had not shown others what later would be revealed to me.

Several weeks passed. I still had no understanding of why the Lord placed these two verses on my heart, but I circled and dated them in my Bible. Before too many more months, they would be brought back to my mind.

Life continued without disruption. Then, during one evening at a home group meeting, a visiting speaker turned to me. He addressed me by name, and his words went something like this: "I don't know your situation, if you're married . . . but the Lord's hand is on the door handle."

At that time, I had been born again for about fifteen years and had become active in Christian fellowship. But my husband had made a clear decision to turn back from an earlier commitment to Christ. He also made it clear that belief in God was my choice, not his. He was not antagonistic and socialized with my Christian friends and even assisted my work for the body of Christ.

So, hearing this message from a stranger, you might understand how I interpreted it to mean that God was about to bring my husband back into the fold. But that was not what it meant. Weeks passed with seemingly nothing happening. Then, on Labor Day weekend 1979, I woke up to a new reality.

On that Sunday morning, just as I did each week, I picked up three of my grandkids who lived next door and went to church. My cellphone rang on the way home. I still remember the very spot along the road where I answered the call.

"I need to tell you before you get home, that I don't live there anymore."

It was my husband's voice. I didn't answer. I couldn't speak. I hung up.

When I arrived home, all his things were gone—clothes, books, items connected to his hobbies. Nothing was left but shattered dreams. I later learned that he had been arranging his exit for some time. He had rented an apartment in the area and later told me he had a friend who had "traveled that road" with him.

What do you do when a dream, like a morning mist, evaporates before your eyes? What I did was seek God. I didn't ask "why?" I asked "what?"

What do I do now?

I believe it was the Lord's answer for me to revisit journal entries, to look at what I had been reading, and what I had been underlining in my Bible. While doing these things, I came back to that Scripture in Jeremiah. The Lord had drawn a red line. His hand had opened the door, but it was not to bring my husband in. My acceptance of this new reality didn't happen quickly, and the pain didn't just dissolve, but eventually I saw life in a new perspective.

When a chapter closes in our story, another one begins. Just as with the birth of a child, there is struggle and pain in that process. My physical birth required intervention and was by C-section. There are many times that the Lord intervenes in our lives to bring us into new beginnings.

The pain of that new beginning is but a memory. I now smile as I recall the events of that time because the joy of the moment eclipses the pain of the past.

I tell my story, not to revisit the scene, but to encourage those who even now are trying to pick up the pieces of shattered dreams. There is a way through the fog. The light will shine on your path. You, too, will smile and find that new beginning. And, oh I beg you, please never forget there is One who has seen your pain. He is waiting to reveal to you the way, the truth, and the life.

Let me end this account of one chapter of my life with one more verse from the Bible, this time from the prophet Isaiah.

Behold, I am doing a new thing; now it springs forth, do you not perceive it? I will make a way in the wilderness and rivers in the desert. Isaiah 43:19 (ESV)

I'll Take Sprinkles

Add a little whimsy to your
Morning every day.
Take time to find some fun
stuff

As you go along your way.
When you laugh at trouble and
folks
Think you absurd
Remind them, joy and laughter,
too,

Are sprinkled through the Word
Let them see your freedom
As on Jesus you rely:
We only need call out His name
And He is by our side.
Give to Him your "tiresome,"
your "weary" and
your pain.
Make "whimsy" your umbrella

When
the world is filled
with Rain.

Eileen Frost

Welcomed into Healing
Rachel Plumley

I would rather host a half-dozen boys for pizza and a nerf gun battle than sit at my writing desk alone. Loneliness was a major barrier to my childhood dream of writing a book. My extrovert personality was more than just a longing for companionship. To be alone was to face the task of writing the hard things, the unflattering scenes of my memoir. I trudged through this process for almost a decade without much support.

When our fourth military move brought us back to my hometown, I discovered a writers group was meeting at the church where we were married. I attended for at least a year before I read even a simple writing exercise from our five-minute prompt. Why was this so hard when I love public speaking? My major in college was communication! Why did I care so much what this room of writers thought about me?

I discovered that the loneliness problem was deeper than needing friends, even than needing affirmation. I needed healing.

It was difficult to write the true story of surviving domestic violence because my wounds were not yet healed. Shame shackled me in shadows. Doubts about my worthiness still plagued me. *Is my story worthy of even one reader's time? What will they think of me if I tell the whole story?*

Our group leader invited me to a small group in her home. She lit candles, played classical music, and served hot tea. A few ladies from writers group arrived, and we pecked away at our keyboards. Some scratched on notepads. All were cozy and inspired! I took a chance and opened my heart to these ladies.

Finally, one Tuesday night at writers group, I was brave enough to read aloud. Another month, I wrote a devotional for the group. No one threw tomatoes. In fact, they smiled and thanked me. The husband of one of my best friends started attending, and more men joined the group. I learned that I could trust them, too. Trusting men is hard, so this speaks to their character.

It's risky to be vulnerable. To trust someone with your story is profoundly healing, especially when they love you even more once the story is told.

The moment I realized I could trust my writing mentor was when she told me her story. This fueled the fire in me to complete my memoir, not just hide it in my desk. Parts of my story were so traumatic that I decided to try EMDR (Eye Movement Desensitization and Reprocessing) therapy to process. God guided me through this deeper layer of healing. Now I sleep well, experience no flashbacks, and think more clearly.

Isn't it wonderful that God designed love to heal even the greatest traumas of our past. Our writers group members live out love as we do life together. We attend each other's book launches. We cheer for each small and large accomplishment. We celebrate a poem written, a query submitted, an eBook for sale! We edit and proof. We're beta readers for each other. We meet on Zoom for accountability. We buy each other's books, write reviews and social media posts. We pray together. God's love is poured out within our group!

I set out looking for a writers group and found a home, healing, and lifelong friends. God is so good to place the lonely in families! My home will continue to swarm with boys, bikes, Legos, barbells, and basketballs. Now I love the quiet moments I can sneak to my desk and write.

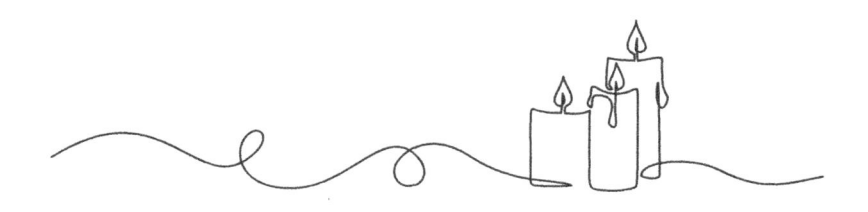

A Writer's Prayer

Lord, I release all the overwhelm, all the fear of "not-enough" or "too-much-ness" that I feel when it comes to putting pen to page.

Thank You that You give me peace . . . and Your presence when I am overwhelmed.

Word made flesh, You dwelt among us. May my words be pleasing to You. Use me as You will.

I pray that my words will bring hope and inspire others. May the words You give me be used for my healing and for the benefit of others. And may the healing that comes through my writing be a blessing to those You have called.

In Jesus' name, Amen.

Jennifer Napier

Questions for Guided Journaling

Do you find it difficult to share your work with your family and friends? Why?

_____
_____
_____
_____
_____
_____
_____
_____
_____
_____
_____
_____
_____
_____

Jesus said to them, "A prophet is not without honor except in his own town, among his relatives and in his own home."
Mark 6:4 (NIV)

"When I face the desolate impossibility of writing 500 pages, a sick sense of failure falls on me, and I know I can never do it. Then gradually, I write one page and then another. One day's work is all I can permit myself to contemplate."

JOHN STEINBECK

Part 3: Determination

... being confident of this very thing, that He who has begun a good work in you will complete it until the day of Jesus Christ;

Philippians 1:6 (NKJV)

A Virtual Slap for the Bogeyman

Evelyn J. Wagoner

Don't tell me you haven't wanted to do it too—just reach right through your monitor into cyberspace and slap someone for something he/she's written. I read a blog post a while ago, and I so wished I could do just that. I envisioned this fellow sitting at his computer, flabbergasted to see my hand reaching out of his monitor and just slapping the tar out of him. (Slapping the tar out of someone—that's a Southern thing, y'all.) I got an enormous feeling of satisfaction from the look of stunned surprise I imagined on his face.

I suppose you need a little backstory, don't you?

It started with an email I received from the most gifted writer I've ever read. I am NOT exaggerating. Y'all, this girl can write. Oh, she'll hem and haw and blush and want to crawl under a chair because I've dared say that OUT LOUD, but it's true. I'll call her WG here (Wonder Girl) so I won't embarrass her further. So, WG emails me the link to an article she's read, and she says if this guy, who's already a published author, is ready to give up, what is she even doing? How can she ever get her story out there and read?

Geez.

At that time, WG had almost finished the first draft of an amazing novel. Her rough draft is, oh, maybe a gazillion times better than most authors' tenth drafts. (I've been a bit concerned about electrocuting myself from drooling into my keyboard reading the section she emails me.) And this article has her doubting herself?

Oooooh, was I angry. Not at her, mind you. At the Bogeyman.

Don't get me wrong. This isn't the first time she's doubted herself—and she's not alone. We writers doubt ourselves every day. Pretty much every other moment. According to Patricia Hermes, a writer I heard at a writers conference, it doesn't matter how many times you've been published. Patricia is the author of over 50 books, and she still thinks everything she writes is crap. She never thinks she has anything to say or that anyone will want to read what she writes. And she swears every writer—published or not—feels the same way.

Okay. So WG and I are in good company. That pretty much means discouragement comes naturally to writers. If that's the case, we certainly don't need any more of it, do we? We have a hard enough time admitting we're writers. Every so often in the group I belong to, we stand up and say, "My name is __, and I'm a writer." Yeah, I know that sounds like we're at one of those other meetings. Well, believe me, it's that tough for some of us to say the words.

The writer who disturbed us so listed "demotivators" in his article. How's that for depressing? I'm constantly searching for guest speakers to inspire and motivate our writers and here, in an article about publishing today, this guy is handing out demotivators. Sigh.

Now he does make a couple of points I can't argue with. Yes, in this new world of easy self- and e-publishing, the market is flooded with books. [Millions of new books are published every year. Literally.] And, yes, it seems that it's getting harder and harder to get published traditionally. So, if you do manage to get a book out there, what are the odds anyone will read it?

Another point he makes—and this is the one that truly rattled WG—is that most writers feel writing is something we do, not only because we enjoy it, but because we believe it is a gift from God, and we should use this gift. I agree. How many times have I quoted Leo Buscaglia? "Your talent is God's gift to you. What you do with it is your gift to God."

But then the writer goes on to say that Christian writers have been "bashed over the head about not 'preaching' in our fiction," that we're being told to only let the example of our characters' lives and the lives of the authors themselves be the Gospel message. And if he writes "fiction that takes [him] a year of hard work, goes largely unnoticed by a majority of the reading audience, does nothing to further the Gospel and has no lifelong effect on the reader, then what am I doing? Probably just wasting my time." He asks, "What good is fiction? How does it spread the Gospel? How does it accomplish the work of Christ?" He touts that "faith writing in fiction is practically worthless."

Gee. Ever heard of Francine Rivers? What about *The Chronicles of Narnia*? *The Screwtape Letters*? How about *Pilgrim's Progress*? *Hinds' Feet on High Places*? The *Left Behind* series? Peretti's *This*

Present Darkness? (And I'd proudly and confidently add WG's novel, and—hopefully—my own, to the list.)

In *Write His Answer,* Marlene Bagnull says, *"In light of eternity, low pay and rejection slips mean nothing if even one life is touched."* And while it would be so gratifying to receive high pay and never again be faced with a rejection slip, Marlene is right. "Words are sacred. They deserve respect. If you get the right ones, in the right order, you can nudge the world a little." (Tom Stoppard) Nudging the world would be an incredible accomplishment. But, in truth, having even a small impact on one life would be an amazing triumph . . . and well worth all the hours bent over a keyboard.

But I guess the main reason I wanted to slap the Bogeyman was simply because we writers (or anyone for that matter) don't need any more discouragement. We deal with enough self-doubt, misgivings, hardships, trials, setbacks, tribulations, (see your Thesaurus for additional words).

Besides, my favorite Writer (not WG this time, but THE Writer), says the *"words of the godly encourage many . . ."* (Proverbs 10:21) and that we are to *"encourage each other and build each other up."* (1 Thessalonians 5:11)

So hug a writer—or anyone who might be a bit discouraged—and say something sweet today. (Remember, "You are not a dork" is not an affirmation.)

And, honestly, I've never slapped anyone.

Dying

Be brave
gaze from your shadow
grace goes with dismay
you are not dead
you live to treasure
the breath of solace
to know
your fleeting pulse
will again flower
in heaven.

DM Frech

He Knew the Cock Would Crow

Jessica Snook

At the end of a busy day, what do you see when you look in the mirror? Some admire themselves as they review their day's successes, but you may see your fatigue, the tension in your face, the weight you carry over the day's failures.

Irritability at work. Impatience with the kids. Road rage at the stop light. Succumbing to gossip. Walking past a person in need, whether from embarrassment or being weary. Avoiding an apology. Not doing what a follower of Christ should have done. Sometimes the strikes against us can seem so numerous and overwhelming, we wonder if we will ever be the people God intends. How could we not disappoint Him? Sometimes the mirror seems to mock us in our weakness.

Take heart! God knew our failures were coming. He knew that the flesh would win today. That temper would take the reins. Cowardice would conquer courage. And He knew how low it would make us feel.

Jesus also knew the cock would crow.

The Lord knew that Simon, called Peter, would fail Him. A man who was one of Jesus' closest friends—and was commended for recognizing early that Jesus is the Christ—denied even knowing Jesus. And he did it within sight of his Lord, who was able to hear and look the apostle straight in the eye as the cock crowed with his betrayal. Scripture tells us Peter was tormented by his failure, that he went away and wept bitterly.

But remember, Jesus knew the cock would crow.

From the beginning of time, Jesus knew the cock would crow. Before the formation of the earth, He knew that Simon Peter would fail, and He knew that we would fail as well. In spite of this knowledge, despite what would come the night of Simon Peter's betrayal, Jesus said to this man: *"And I tell you that you are Peter, and on this rock I will build My church . . . "* (Matthew 16:18a NIV) You can almost hear the pride in our Lord's voice as He speaks in this passage. When Jesus foretold of Peter's denial, He assured the apostle that the failure would pass. He gives clear instructions to move forward afterward and that Peter should then strengthen his brothers. And Peter was the one chosen to lead the early Church.

Yes, you will fail. You may fail daily. But God chose you and called you by name, despite your failures, because you have the potential of a warrior. That He would use you to be His hands and feet and voice, to conquer mountains in His name, to become the light on the hill and point the way to Christ.

In 2 Corinthians 12, Paul says God humbled him with an illness or other flaw that tormented him. He prayed to have his suffering removed, but God's answer was "no." In verse nine He says, *"My grace is sufficient for you, for My power is made perfect in weakness."* Paul's response becomes, *"Therefore I will boast all the more gladly of my weaknesses, so that the power of Christ may rest upon me."* (NIV)

Our failures could be the catalyst that teaches us to reach for God's mercy and grace and shows others what is possible through Him. Conscious reliance on God allows Him to work in our lives and demonstrate His power in the midst of our weakness.

It is God's strength within us that creates a usable vessel. There is relief in the knowledge that the battle is not ours but the Lord's. He can and will use us despite everything we see in the mirror. He chose us intentionally, from the beginning of time, even knowing that our own personal cock would crow.

Song to the Weary

Oh, dearest child of Mine
You sit so weary, weeping.
The toil has been long and lonely,
You fear resolve is seeping.

You've stayed strong for, oh, so long,
With all these burdens, stood so tall.
Continuing to move forward,
But so certain you will fall.

Yet, through it all, My treasured child,
Breathe in deep and feel Me near,
Sit quiet and know that I AM, little one,
Even when gripped by those talons of fear.

Compared to My size, My strength, My Word,
Your enemies are but dust and smoke.
And when they try to pierce your heart,
Remember there was nothingness before I spoke.

I am He who aligned the planets.
I am He who determined your worth.
I am He who covers your frailness,
And directs your steps on this earth.

You are the one I died to repurchase.
You are the one I chose before time.
You are the one I have given a purpose
That will be known when the moment is right.

Now reach for the courage I give you;
Lift your eyes (yes, you can dare!)
You will see you are covered in armor,
And a sword is waiting near.

You have feared the coldness of failure,
But feel, My breath is warm
As I stand as a Lion above you.
And around you My army is formed.

So, rise as I make your feet weightless,
My angels will cover your way.
You are a soldier of Zion, dear child,
And we'll win your battle today.

Jessica Snook

A Lesson in Love and Determination
Billie Montgomery / Cook

Do you remember "BUPPIES"? Those **B**lack, **U**rban **P**rofessionals that young black people over the age of 25 aspired to become? Keith, my husband, and I held that title for about five minutes. We became some of the "BUFFIES"—**B**ankrupt, **U**nemployed and **F**oreclosed during the years of 1995 to 2001.

In August 1994, I learned that my job at Old Dominion University as Advisor to College of Business freshman students would end. The College of Business decided to close the Advising Center (where I worked) and go to Faculty Advising. It was a decision we fought against, and the college would decide about five years later that, yep, we were right, and they shouldn't have closed it. It seems that not every faculty member had student advising as a priority in their academic life.

August found me unemployed with few prospects. There had been a few offers on campus, but those had to be refused because, as the mother of two elementary school age children and wife of a struggling Baptist preacher/pastor, I had very little freedom. The saving grace (ain't God good?) to my being unemployed was that it meant I had just made the five-year mark that June at ODU and was considered "vested" in the State's Retirement System.

One evening in early December 1994, Keith departed for what would become a life-altering board meeting at the church. He returned to announce that he had resigned from the church effective the first Sunday of January 1995. BUFFIE world, here we come!

The TV show *In Living Color* was comical testament to the fact that it was possible for people to work three to five "jobs" at any given time. Keith and I weren't laughing. By day, he became a substitute teacher, a home-bound instructor (a "visiting" teacher for students in the public school system who are out of school due to illness), and, by night, a 7/11 employee. On the weekends, Keith did security work at warehouses and public utility locations. I also taught home-bound students, tutored for a program, and taught orientation classes at Tidewater Community College, Norfolk campus.

A few months of this daily grind proved perilous to our family life. Keith was exhausted, and I insisted that he quit the 7/11 job. He did, gladly, but it still meant that additional income was needed.

Keith replaced that with another day job—working part-time for the Norfolk City Sheriff's Department. In that position, he picked up work release inmates from the jobs that they had around the city and returned them at night to the jail. He absolutely loved it, and the Sheriff's department loved him! In time, while doing that job, he was invited to apply as a sheriff's deputy. He did and was accepted. He then went to the sheriff's academy for training.

We lost our home (that's the foreclosed part) in the spring of 1997. Understand that we had gone for 23 months *not* being able to pay/afford our mortgage. In other words, our Heavenly Father had provided us with one month shy of two years of housing—still in our foreclosed home—and not homeless. We knew the end was coming and that we would have to move, but where? Once again, God provided by placing us in a very small house with an unbelievable rent! We would live there until 2001, when we were able to purchase our forever home.

Meanwhile, our children (we had two—a girl and a boy) were growing up fast, especially our daughter, Jeanina. When she was in middle school, the "stories" started and I was terrified. Almost daily, Jeanina would come home with stories about which boys, but girls especially, were fighting each other and the petty reasons for the fights ("he/she/I said" etc.). However, the pregnancy stories really freaked me out. Yes, middle school girls getting pregnant, having abortions, etc. What do you do with those kinds of stories, issues, and concerns *after* you pray and beg Jesus not to allow you to become a policeman over your one and only daughter?

As an intelligent and educated mother, I did the intelligent and educated thing: I sought out books that I could give her to help her during this difficult stage and passage of growth. The books about puberty proved helpful, and she read those and shared them with her girlfriends for hours! The books, *What Your Mother Never Told You About Sex,* by Dr. Hilda Hutcherson, a black female gynecologist, and *Our Bodies, Ourselves*, by the Boston Women's Health Collective, were gold.

I had hit a home run with the biological and physical side of growing up but the spiritual part was clearly lacking. Back to the bookstore. There were quite a few good books, written primarily by young, white youth ministers but next to nothing for a developing Black female. The idea came to me (the Holy Spirit?) to write Jeanina a letter, outlining all the things I wanted her to know, not only about what it meant to grow up Black and female in a country that didn't value her or her history, but what God's Word said about and to her. When she was about 13, the letter started. With each new "story" from school, the letter got longer and longer.

It wasn't a book; it was simply a letter—a lengthy one but still a letter. And definitely not a book. I didn't write books. I wrote plays and had written (and produced) quite a few plays for drama ministries for two churches. By the time Jeanina turned 16, the "letter" was finished. I printed it out, placed it in a box, gift wrapped it with pink paper and bows, and presented it to her on her birthday. I was proud of it and felt confident I had covered just about all the subjects I thought were important and crucial for her moving forward as a young Black woman of God. She was less than impressed. She wanted a car, not a book. I was devastated but dealt with it. Days later, I overheard her reading passages of the letter to one of her girlfriends. My goal had been accomplished, and I was happy and satisfied.

Meanwhile, Keith had been "on the sidelines" working every day as a sheriff's deputy in the jail but watching me work on the "letter" and seeing Jeanina's response. I was still working at TCC but encountering problems with the new supervisor for the orientation classes. We tended to clash over our different visions for the class. Up to that time, all the instructors had been given free rein to cover specific topics in our own creative ways. The new supervisor wanted each and every class to be taught the same exact way. I was miserable, but we needed the money.

At one point, Keith sat me down, told me to quit the TCC job, come home, and write the book that was the letter to Jeanina. He said other young Black girls, just like our Jeanina, needed that book. I immediately said, "No," and started the speech that went something like, "I'm not a writer. I just write plays. I can't do that. I'm not that good. You must be crazy to even ask me to consider doing such a thing, especially at this financial juncture in this family." He assured me that we could and would—with the help of Almighty God—live on just his salary for as long as it took me to write the book.

What do you do when someone believes in you, your skills, and your talents more than you believe in yourself? How many times do you hear yourself say, "No, I don't think I can do that" before you just stop saying those words out loud? At what point does your resistance, self-doubt, and fear end? After a week, a month, a year? Two years? Ten? What do you do? You shut up, close your eyes, pray like crazy and dive head first into the "Can I really do this?" pool. To be honest, I had attended quite a few writers conferences and had all the information I needed to get started. I had learned how to research different publishers and how to write query letters. I just had to do it.

I contacted a publisher (Judson Press) who loved the concept of the book. I just needed to re-write it to the "universal daughter" rather than our Jeanina, and come up with a title. We learned that my initial title was already in use by a couple who had a workout video online. I asked my niece, who was in her early 20s and did youth ministry at her church, to read it and give me feedback as well as possible titles.

One Saturday morning, while in the shower (why do we do our best thinking in the shower?), I had the title: *The Real Deal: A Spiritual Guide for Black Teen Girls.* I shared the title with the Acquisitions Editor, Randy Frame, at Judson who loved the title but told me I then had to re-write it (again!) so that the book reflected the title. And I had one month to re-write it. During that month, we lost power for an entire week because of Hurricane Isabel. Despite the obstacles, I did the re-write and God truly blessed! *The Real Deal* became a national bestseller (10,000 books sold for Christian Fiction) and remains (#7) on Judson's top ten of their bestselling books (last count 21,000+ sold).

So, what do you do when you lack confidence or faith in yourself while someone who truly loves you is determined to push you to spread your wings and fly? You listen to them and you trust their judgment over your own. You *do it,* whatever *it* is. And you pray that what they are telling you is truly God inspired and God directed— because it probably is!

Psalm of Trust

My mind turns over in a continual quest to understand the Why's
and How's
But I repent, O Lord,
and *I choose to trust in You.*

I want to taste the tree of knowledge,
But I know its fruit is bitter
For it only gives a false sense of control.
The tree of life is the "unknowing" and part of the mystery of God.
This is where I will rest my weary mind
and *I will choose to trust in You.*

It is all too easy to turn my gaze to the culture's words of
Truth, success, and security.
My eyes become blurry with the sting of confusion.
But I return and set my gaze upon you, O Lord,
for I know your thoughts and ways are higher
and *I choose to trust in You.*

Amy Heilman

Perseverance In the Midst of Rejection

Dr. James R. Boyd

So, you have been rejected. Welcome to the group of successful survivors! Wisdom often results from trying to apply knowledge and finding that sometimes we are not successful. We can learn a lot from such failures. Just don't lose hope.

"Hope itself is like a star—not to be seen in the sunshine of prosperity, and only to be discovered in the night of adversity." (Charles Spurgeon)

Rejection can encourage you to refocus efforts, leading to higher levels of personal success. When you are rejected, it could be due to your lack of clarity about yourself! Begin your approach by focusing on the road ahead. Consider Philippians 4:6-7, *Be anxious for nothing, but in everything by prayer and supplication, with thanksgiving, let your request be known to God: and the peace of God, which surpasses all understanding, will guard your hearts and minds through Christ Jesus.* (NKJV) That assurance will bring you peace and help you to move forward past rejection.

Four actions can be effective:

A. Know Who You Are
Coming to Him as to a living stone, rejected indeed by men, but chosen by God and precious, you also, as living stones, are being built up a spiritual house, a holy priesthood, to offer up spiritual sacrifices acceptable to God through Jesus Christ. (1 Peter 2:4-5 NKJV)

For we are His workmanship, created in Christ Jesus for good works, which God prepared beforehand that we should walk in them. (Ephesians 2:10 NKJV)

You are precious and worthy, and so is the work you do.

B. Explore the Root of the Adversity
What is the cause of the adversity? Consider conditions leading to rejection, and document details regarding it. Communicate directly with the party involved.

C. Consider Your Part
Could they be correct to resist or reject you? Do you have a personal or emotional bias? Are you honestly considering what you have done that led to the problem?

D. Focus on Others
Helping others could help you, and take your mind off your problems.

E. Reset Your Position
Remove any obstacles to communications and progress, starting with yourself. Step back, and don't get personal. Detach from the emotion, pressure, and confusion.

Reduce elements that prevent you from focusing on or accomplishing your goal. That includes concern about progress. Build it strong. Quality takes time.

Reenergize by stepping back and resting. Slow down, pray, and pump peace into your life. Once you have mastered yourself, you can master anything that faces you (see Proverbs 16:32).

Remember why you first began the task. Adversity comes when you take on any worthy goal.

Reconstruct and review the plans you made, considering other opportunities available now. Adjust, reorganize, and reconstruct your thinking, using trusted counselors to discuss the future and your best steps to move ahead.

Where there is no counsel, the people fall; but in the multitude of counselors there is safety. (Proverbs 11:14 NKJV)

Understand that adversity is meant to strengthen and test you for future rewards (see James 1:12).

Perseverance is the foundation for success. Use rejection to work through it.

> "There is no substitute for hard work."
> Thomas A. Edison

A Writer's Prayer

DEAR LORD, May I have Your grace to finish and submit a work for publication.
May I be blessed by You to get Your message to the world.
You give me tools—teach me to use them without excuses.
Help me focus and complete what You ask me to do.
To help others in their struggles in life.
To guide others to You and give them hope and love.

We all need Your love, Lord, every day.
Show us the way.
Take us to the next step.
Help us look to You always, so we can do Your work.

In Jesus' name, Amen.

Mary Stasko

"The One who hovers over creation lives inside me. I need never say to the blank page, 'I got nothing.'"
(Anon)

Photography by DM Frech

Questions for Guided Journaling

Are you willing to persevere despite rejection, or do you expect the Lord to somehow make it easy?

---

*Even if my father and mother abandon me,
the Lord will hold me close.*
Psalm 27:10 (NLT)

"Every step, every choice, every action or inaction in my life prepared me, propelled me to become the writer I am becoming. Through Grace, my writing lights candles in darkness leaving a trail for those who might pass this way. For me, writing is the thing I Can't Not do. Where God will lead my words and my heart I do not yet know, but it is clear, this is the thing to which I have been called."

Scott Adams

PROCESS

*Many plans are in a man's mind,
but it is the LORD's purpose for him
that will stand (be carried out).*
Proverbs 19:21 (AMP)

Do These Four Things
Dylan West

Though the canon of Scripture stands complete, God still needs writers. And if He's called us to write, He wants us to succeed. As the Author of the bestselling book of all time, He's plenty qualified to help us. In fact, His book gives advice on the matter if we know where to look. Though the Bible isn't a writer's handbook, it guides all who work for God. That includes storytellers. Let's see how its principles apply to our craft.

Start Now
He who observes the wind will not sow,
And he who regards the clouds will not reap.
In the morning sow your seed,
And in the evening do not withhold your hand;
For you do not know which will prosper,
Either this or that,
Or whether both alike will be good.
(Ecclesiastes 11:4,6 NKJV)

As with farming, chance plays a part in a writer's success. We need to be okay with that and keep writing anyway. We do the work knowing some things are beyond our control, including the results.

Don't wait for perfect conditions to start writing and selling books. When I sit down at my word-weary keyboard, I tell God, "I don't know if this session will result in a masterpiece or messy pieces, but here I am. Keep me in this chair until I'm done, and help me write along with You."

I don't have to feel inspired to start typing. Just like I don't have to feel peppy to drive to the farmers market, set up my table, and sell books. Each event is its own species. I can't guess how many shoppers will show up, whether the weather will drive them off, or if foot traffic will flow away from my table because my nearest vendors left early. When I speak with passing shoppers, I can't control their mood, budget, or buying preferences. Maybe the dog they're walking drags them to the food truck. Or their kids suddenly want to go home. I determine none of those things.

All I can do is show up and call out. The rest is up to God. In my one hundred vendor events so far, I've never failed to sell at least enough to cover the vendor fee. Sometimes I sell over four hundred dollars of books in one afternoon. On my best day, I sold forty-six books in seven hours. One shopper even bought my book with two hundred dollars and told me to keep the change!

It pays to show up. And to do that, we have to get started.

Be Faithful

Authors want to write something valuable and spread it to everyone. God wants this, too, but insists that we work for it.

. . . Whoever sows sparingly will also reap sparingly, and whoever sows bountifully will also reap bountifully. 2 Corinthians 9:6 (ESV)

Translated for the writer, this might read, "Whoever publishes sparingly will also sell sparingly, and whoever publishes bountifully will also sell bountifully." The long startup period makes a writing career hard to break into. Most writers slog through years of throwaway novels before they publish their debut. Then it takes a train of releases before they can cover the mortgage as an author. It's like becoming a doctor, without the residency and the cadavers. Well, if you're a mystery author, you might be bonesawing into bodies for research. Anyhow . . .

Well done, good and faithful servant! You have been faithful with a few things; I will put you in charge of many things . . . (Matthew 25:23b NIV)

To make a good book, we have to get a thousand little things right. It takes a diligent person to make such a product. And it takes time to become that person. Many days of saying "no" to other activities and "yes" to writing. This whole affair is an act of faith. I wouldn't sink nonrefundable hours at my desk if I didn't believe it would pay off. When I write, I know the following things happen:
- My book gets written;
- My writing skill improves;
- I obey God when I use the gift He entrusted to me.

If writing a quality book wasn't enough, I also have to sell it. For some, this requires more faith than the writing. Many authors don't want to talk to shoppers, thinking themselves bad at sales or preferring to stay at home and write. "If only someone else would magic my books into the loving arms of happy readers!" they say. For a lucky few, this is the case. Stephen King can stay home, and his books will keep selling.

But you're not Stephen King. And neither am I . . . at least not yet. I keep checking my face for those bushy eyebrows of his. When those finally come in, I know my sales will, too. For now, I must go out and sell. In fact, I get to sell. Who better to talk to shoppers than children of God? I get to meet new people and speak truth to them. Giving them my attention is an act of love that may help them as much as my books will. Plus, I get to pet the cute dogs they bring to my outdoor markets!

When I table up at local events, I know these things happen:
- Many will hear about my books;
- Some will buy my books;
- A few will be transformed by my books.

I go to events knowing, just knowing, I'm bound to meet my next biggest fan. That keeps me excited to sell. It makes me want to be faithful to do the little things.

Trust God to Help You

Commit your works to the Lord, and your thoughts will be established. A man's heart plans his way, but the Lord directs his steps. (Proverbs 16:3,9 NIV)

When God establishes your thoughts, you will smash through writer's block and stomp all over the memory of it. Let God guide your ideas and show you how to break your big project into the right steps. Worried readers won't like the finished product? Ask God to send you critique partners. Which brings me to the next item . . .

Get Your Work Critiqued

Where there is no counsel, the people fall; But in the multitude of counselors there is safety. (Proverbs 11:14 NKJV)

Rebuke a wise man, and he will love you. Give instruction to a wise man, and he will be still wiser; Teach a just man, and he will increase in learning. (Proverbs 9:8b,9 NKJV)

Long before I started *Scribes' Descent*, I went on nightly prayer walks, asking for someone to help me with my writing. I begged friends and coworkers to give me feedback on my prior novel, but nobody gave comments I found helpful.

A year later, I became a NASA contractor at the Langley Research Center in Hampton, VA. There I met a system administrator named

Philip Nelson. I went to him when I needed a web server for an application I was building. Gradually, I realized he was a Christian and a fellow fiction lover. Not only that, he'd published his own collection of faith-based short stories, all of which were sci-fi or fantasy!

I sent him a rough draft of *A Signet Forever*—the novel I wrote before *Scribes' Descent*. His comments got me unstuck and revealed big flaws in my storytelling. Five years later, he began giving extensive feedback for the Scribes series at every stage of the project. And he's continued doing so even today. His name tops the acknowledgments page for every book I publish.

Philip was the answer to my prayers.

God didn't stop there. In 2018, I discovered Scribophile (https://scribophile.com) and exchanged critiques with other authors. Over the next four and a half years I wrote 420,000 words of critique, spanning four hundred chapters of various novels. In return, I received over 550 critiques from 350 authors for *Scribes' Descent*. I catalogued 2,500 useful comments and spent another year acting on them. I kept revising and reposting fixes until others consistently told me they couldn't find anything to comment on.

"This book is ready," I kept hearing. "Where can I buy this?"
When I published my book, I did it with full confidence. And when I call out to shoppers at sales events today, I do so knowing *Scribes' Descent* had survived four years of trench warfare and earned the praise of critique partners and beta readers.

Getting feedback may sound easy, but some of it crushed my ribs in ways a 300-pound barbell never could. Some critiquers can be hurtful little imps, and I verged on tears as I wondered if I was wasting my time. But I made myself sift through all my harshest feedback for whatever truth I could find and act on that. I knew a wise man loves rebuke. "God, help me be a wise man," I prayed.

I'm glad I did. So are my readers.

Start now. Be faithful. Trust God to help you. Get your work critiqued. If you grew up hearing three-point sermons, my list of four things may have you twitching. Feel free to combine items one and two into a single point. I won't mind.

Whatever the numbering involved, have these principles worked for me? I'll give you the numbers and let you decide.

In my first two years as a self-published author, I have:
- Sold 1,901 books across three titles;
- Built my newsletter email list to 2,125 subscribers;
- Earned over $21,000 in revenue and $8,700 in profit;
- Received 99 ratings and 90 reviews for *Scribes' Descent* on Amazon.

Not exactly New York Times Bestselling numbers, but they're a decent start. And now for the victories you won't find in spreadsheets:
- One of my fans has read *Scribes' Descent* eight times so far.
- A nine-year-old boy has written fanfiction of my work.
- I inspired another young boy to become a writer when he grows up.
- I encouraged an author friend to start vending at in-person events, where she has now sold hundreds of books.

I don't remember exactly what I prayed during my prayer walks so long ago, but the following is what I pray now. May the Lord answer you as He's been answering me:

When I sit down to write, I sow Your seed.
Father, fertilize them with Your imagination.
When I edit, be my vinedresser. Pull weeds of cliché and brambles of excess.
Leave only words that bend the heart in Your direction.
When I swap critiques, give me safety in Your counselors. Let me hear correction gladly and give it back with kindness. Help the iron of my pen sharpen that of another.
When I leave my desk and stagger out into the sun, I cradle my books in my arms. In a world of busy people, God, lead me to readers. Readers who want books just like mine.
I will not observe the wind.
I will not regard the clouds.
For no matter the weather, I'll sow the seed You've given me.
Morning and evening, I will not withhold my hand.
I'll be faithful with little, so You can trust me with much
Until the author in You becomes an author in me, and Your words climb into the ears of all who will listen.

Gratitude

Mary Stasko

Thanksgiving means gratitude, and gratitude can help you as a writer. God wants you to write and will give you direction and inspiration.

Start off by finding a good notebook—one you like and that makes you want to fill its pages. Treat yourself to a good pen in your favorite color to keep with your journal. Place it somewhere where you would most likely take a few minutes to write—at your bedside, beside your favorite chair, etc. Someplace quiet is helpful. When would be the best time to write? Perhaps at the end of the day when you can write about how thankful you are for the things that happened that day. If nothing comes to mind, write about the past or the future. Write as often as you can—daily, if possible, but at least three times a week. Mark your writing days on your calendar.

You can begin each entry by saying something like, "I am thankful for..." Or write about something that made you happy. Be aware of the emotions that come from the writing.

You can write about others you appreciate and why. You will feel more connected and accomplish more.

Remember to let God help you as you write. Say a prayer before you begin, and focus on your blessings. That positive energy will flow, and your thoughts will be expressed with more confidence. Doing this before bed will help you sleep better.

Write for yourself. There's no need to worry about rejection. Be true to yourself, and tell the stories you need to tell. Find your unique voice and write in the style that comes naturally. No one can tell the story better than you can.

Set short- and long-term goals. Review them when needed, and make changes if necessary, so that you can continue to be encouraged.

Be kind to yourself. Accept the love and support of others.
And remember, God is good all the time. All the time, God is good.

Advice to Struggling Writers

Elizabeth Green

Sometimes you'll find yourself struggling with your writing. Don't give in to fear! Don't let shame or condemnation grip your mind. Struggle is a visitor who shows up occasionally to plague all writers.

To get back on track:

Keep your writing gear ready and in place so that it's easy to grab and get going again.

Step away for a while. Do something inspirational like text a message to encourage someone else.

Go for a walk. Enjoy nature and God's creations. Sights and sounds will ignite your creativity, focus, and hope.

Talk with the Holy Spirit about ideas and writing assignments. Then, LISTEN, LISTEN, LISTEN. WRITE, WRITE, WRITE!

Janxiety

Karen McSpadden

I love the dictionary. I love dignified words like *demure* and *assemblage*, romantic words like *diaphanous* or *gossamer*, and tiny, perky words like *sprocket* and *tink*. It is a particular pet peeve of mine when a blog or Facebook post mashes up perfectly useful words for no reason.

So, I'm here to talk about Janxiety.

But first—tell me, don't you kind of hate that word? I kind of hate that word. It's a senseless social media smash-up of two perfectly useful words—January and anxiety—and it's laboriously cute, like a glitter-covered poodle in a bunny suit. Are our digital lives so frenetic that we must describe all concepts in single-word catchphrases?

I digress.

Janxiety is a phrase coined to cover that general malaise of the soul that often settles in with January like a winter cold. (Or, if you're in my house, it's accompanied by an actual winter cold that won't leave and cycles from person to person like an unpleasant game of telephone. The winner gets a 103-degree fever and a sore throat. But I digress. Again.)

Janxiety is what's waiting for you after the ball drops, after the Christmas decorations are boxed up and the family has gone back over the river and through the woods. *Janxiety* is the feeling you get when you have who knows how many holiday credit card bills and who knows how many extra pounds hanging around the usual places. (Just put the skinny jeans up till March. Trust me.) It's a dash of frustration, a sprinkle of stress, a side of worry, and a long hard look at the gap between where we are and where we want to be. After a month-long celebration of the Incarnation, a breathtaking vista of heavenly wonder, we're back in the half-frozen mud, wondering why we're falling asleep in church, and why it's so hard to find ten minutes to read our Bible.

In other words, if Christmas is a caffeine rush, *Janxiety* is the crash.

So what's the cure? Another holiday? The stores are already filling up with Valentine's cards and candies at a rate that frankly makes my teeth ache. We need the long, boring weeks of January.

They are like a cup of black coffee after a fancy dessert—something to cleanse the palate before the next societal sugar high. But knowing something's good for us doesn't make it taste any better. (I hate black coffee, by the way.)

Then maybe the cure is to solve all those problems you found hiding under the fake snow and leftover Christmas wrapping paper. Pay off the credit cards. Unearth the treadmill. Buy a pretty planner and a fancy pen. Go to bed at a decent hour instead of staying up past midnight taking quizzes to find out which Disney Princess Hairstyle fits your personality. (Maybe that's just *my* problem.) You could sign up for a Bible study, choose a memory verse plan, and volunteer for that nursery shift the children's director has been looking to fill. A few schedule tweaks, a little self-denial, and the new year will be off to a proper start. This could be The Year you get things right. Or at least remember to sort your laundry properly. (Again, maybe that one is just me.)

Only, I don't think we need any of that.

Christmas is a wide-angle shot, a sweeping panorama across millennia of hope and glory. (Do you hear cellos when I say that? I do.) January—and if we're honest, almost *every* day of almost *every* other month—is a relentless close-up. The camera zooms in for a painfully tight view of the cracks in our lives. But it is through those same cracks that glory and hope, though almost invisible, are making their way through every part of creation. Including our mundane mid-winter lives. That's where we live. The new kingdom that Christ has *already* won for us and for the world is not yet fully seen. But the wonder and hope and cello-music-goosebumps are still there, if we give ourselves moments to experience them. And to do that, we can't be desperately waiting for the next Big Day or filling up a to-do list with Twenty Steps to Better. We have to stop where we are *today* and look around.

Which is why I have a chair.

Actually, I have several, but I love a *specific* chair in a *specific* corner of the living room. That chair is mine. To have one's own chair is a common and quite delicious pleasure. I don't get to sit long—I have three kids—but I can read a page in a book that inspires me, knit a few stitches of a hat, or scribble a paragraph of my next story. I can sip my favorite tea. Some days—okay, *many* days—I'm so tired that I just sit and sigh the same prayer: *Lord, it's not working today, and I don't know how it ever will. Please give me the strength to get up and do one more thing for love's sake. For hope and for Your glory.*

So, if you suffer from Janxiety—at any time of the year—find your chair. Or your table, or your desk, or your corner of the couch. You get the idea. Grab with both hands the things *already* true of you in Christ. Keep hold of them while you face all the *not-yet* places in your life. Small, unglamorous graces are, to my mind, by far the best. Small, ordinary words are more than enough to fill a page.

A Time for Every *Thing*

Penny Hutson

As writers we're told to set specific writing goals, such as write ten pages a day. We're further advised to be consistent and stick to that schedule. Many successful writers from Stephen King to R.L. Stine employ these methods. And of course, we all know that to complete anything, one must spend time working on it .

However, we should also remember what it tells us in Ecclesiastes 3:1. *To every thing there is a season, and a time to every purpose under the heaven.* (KJV)

To me, this means there is a time to write and a time to rest from writing. A little space between us and our writing is invaluable. When we return to it, we're refreshed and can look with new eyes. We may see plot holes, point-of-view errors, or tense shifts previously unnoticed.

This "break" may be an excellent time to read. As most writers know, reading forms the basis of all good writing. How can you expect to write a viable mystery or young adult novel, for example, if you haven't recently lost yourself in a good book? In Stephen King's book *On Writing,* he not only agrees with this advice, but he adds that "if you don't have time to read, you don't have the time (or the tools) to write." Others suggest you read the same genre you're writing. So, if you're writing historical fiction, you should be reading historical fiction at the same time. There is an opposite point of view to not read in the same genre so that you won't be influenced. The point is to read! Maybe there's a book on writing craft that would give your writing a boost or an inspirational book to lift your morale. We should never stop taking time to learn and improve our craft.

Then there is a time for editing, feedback, and rewriting. There is also a time for marketing, querying, networking, and doing research.

The next time you're inclined to berate yourself because you didn't meet your writing goals, take a moment to thank God for what you've already created. Then ask Him to reveal to you what time it is. Are you in the season for writing or resting? Editing or researching? Reading or networking? Maybe it's time to go for a walk, have lunch with a friend, or focus on something other than writing.

Let us remember that Ecclesiastes 3:11 also tells us *He [God] hath made every thing beautiful in His time.* (KJV)

A Writer's Prayer

DEAR LORD, You've helped me sell books in person.
Please help me get better at selling them online.

You've helped me cross-promote my books with new authors.
Please help me do the same with more established ones.

You've given me time to build my writing business.
Please help me manage that time more effectively as it grows.

You've given me a host of minor characters for my books.
Please help me develop them more fully so readers feel more invested in them.

You've trained me in graphics, photography, and video editing.
Please help me make videos that help other authors and widen my audience.

You've sent me hungry readers who love my books.
Please help me find new ways to surprise and delight them in all my future work.

Dylan West

"Be yourself.
Above all, let who you are,
what you are, what you
believe shine through every
sentence you write,
every piece you finish."

John Jakes

Questions for Guided Journaling

Writers typically fall into three categories:
1. Plotters: plan out their stories from beginning to end, working from a detailed outline.
2. Pantsers: start with a vague idea in mind and see where the story takes them, writing "by the seat of their pants."
3. Plantsers: allow deviation from a basic outline if and when inspiration strikes.

Which category describes you best? What are the pros and cons of your approach?

Let not mercy and truth forsake you;
Bind them around your neck,
Write them on the tablet of your heart.
Proverbs 3:3 (NKJV)

"Her mother had taught her that talent is a gift from God, that a writer has a sacred obligation to her Creator to explore the gift with energy and diligence, to polish it, to use it to brighten the landscape of her readers' hearts."

DEAN KOONTZ, FROM *THE TAKING*

RESPONSIBILITY

Arise, for this matter is your responsibility. We also are with you. Be of good courage, and do it.

Ezra 10:4 (NKJV)

In Plain Sight

Evelyn J. Wagoner

I started off the morning by falling. Tripped in the dark and walloped my head against the trunk that nestles against the foot of our antique bed. My husband, the sweet guy I was trying not to awaken, leaped up with the speed and grace of a gazelle with good knees. He was, shall we say, a bit freaked out, yelping, "Honey-honeyhoneyhoney!" then, "Jesus, Jesus, Jesus."

I lay on my side, my head bent at an awkward angle, knees grazed, right hand gripping my left wrist like a vise, chanting, "I'm all right, I'm all right, I'm all right," though I couldn't have sworn it was true. I wasn't quite ready to move, not quite ready to test my body. Though somewhat satisfied my neck wasn't broken, I wasn't sure about my wrist. Before my husband could flip on the light, one thought did emerge coherent. "Cover my butt! Cover my butt!" I cried. I heard a swallowed laugh, but he complied, bending down in the early morning shadows to tug at my nightgown.

It was kind of strange, that fall. Tripping over something I knew was there. You see, that "thing" had been there all week, in the path between my closet and bathroom. I had navigated around it without thought, without effort. It was big and soft. As a co-worker pointed out, I tripped over something soft and collided with something hard (the reverse would have been so much smarter). Why had I stepped out of our closet, tripped, and flown? Who knows?

How many other things have tripped me up on my way to my goals? Things I know are there, things in plain sight. Most of the time that thing is fear, in all its many forms. Fear of rejection, of criticism, of failure, of being thought silly, or stupid, or (fill in the blank). Or the bigger fear of no one reading what I write or checking my posts if I were to ever begin a blog. For years I've allowed so many things to trip me up, to keep me from moving toward what is the essence of who I am, who I dream of being.

The incident got me thinking about the Henry David Thoreau line "Most men lead lives of quiet desperation . . ." Most stop quoting right there. After all, just that much can be enough. It's compelling, and folks can identify. But there's more to that famous quote: " . . . and go to the grave with the song still in them." Now that's a mind-numbing thought. And if I don't buck up and keep putting one foot in front of the other, if I don't look that fear in the eye and make it back down, then it will win, and I will continue to live a life of quiet desperation (though I'm not necessarily so quiet about it. Just ask my husband and friends). My song will go to the grave with me.

Instead, I want to be like Erma Bombeck who said, "When I stand before God at the end of my life, I would hope that I would not have a single bit of talent left and could say, 'I used everything You gave me.'"

All in all, the fall was good for me. My neck and back were a bit sore, my right knee carpet-burned and stiff, my knuckles boxer-bruised (after all, I did "hit the deck," ha ha!), my left wrist was purple, and I dealt with a headache for most of the day. Still, a happy ending, when you consider what could have happened after slamming my head on a vintage chest. And, in the end, I pretty much kept my dignity.

What is tripping you up? Determine to take some small step toward your goal today, toward your dream.

"Enough shovels of earth—a mountain. Enough pails of water—a river." Chinese proverb

A Writer's Prayer

O LORD, open my eyes lest I be blind, and help me reach past my limited understanding. Show me how to write in such a way that Your truth comes through the words of my story.

Let me bring a healing touch to those who have been wounded. Let me open eyes that have been closed, and give me insight on how to plant seeds of hope in the hearts of those who have none.

O God, let me never be afraid to write about the broken places in my own life.

Valerie Fay

The Challenge of Carpe Diem
Confronting the "Coulda," "Shoulda," "Wouldas" of Our Time

Joyce Kirby

Be very careful, then, how you live—not as unwise but as wise, making the most of every opportunity. (Ephesians 5:15-16a NIV) *There is a time for everything, and a season for every activity under the heavens.* (Ecclesiastes 3:1 NIV)

We live in challenging times, don't we? 2020 will probably go down in history as one of the most difficult years ever. With the invasion of the COVID-19 virus, our world and our lives were locked down. It wreaked havoc on each of us in so many ways. We were bombarded by a plethora of emotions that zapped us of energy and took a toll on our creativity, even the very desire to write and pursue our passion.

We will all look back on that time and remember when. Remember when we all had to wear masks; remember when we couldn't find a roll of toilet paper in the store and even Amazon was sold out; remember when we couldn't visit our loved one in the nursing home or hospital; remember when the phrases "social distancing," "curbside pick-up," and "herd immunity" became part of our American vernacular.

Yes, something drastic happened to all of us in the early 2020s—and it impacted every person on this planet. But how are we, as writers, looking at it? What are we seeing in the fallout of the COVID pandemic? I think we were given an old-fashioned object lesson about the proverbial glass: is it half empty or half full? We spent close to three years self-isolating in our homes, protecting ourselves and our loved ones from a heinous virus. At first glance, most of us viewed our glass as half empty. After all, what good came from this pandemic?

The world changed because of this pandemic; America changed. *You* changed. What words would you use to describe yourself today? Anxious? Angry? Stressed? Peaceful? How about Sanguine? Striving? Apathetic? Or maybe you are at the other end of the spectrum describing yourself as Proactive, Productive, Successful, and Happy, reaping the benefits of realizing the goals you had four years ago. Are you closer to Jesus? Are you still a writer?

How do you view the pandemic in the rearview mirror? Is that glass half empty or half full? Are there a lot of shoulda, coulda, wouldas? Things you wish you had done differently or just done period? Are there relationships that could have been healed? Grace that should have been extended; discussions that should have taken place; books that could have been read; a blog, article or book that would have been written had you just seized the day?

Do you look back to 2020 and see how much you squandered God's gift of time? Did you spend time worrying about things you couldn't change, watching TV shows that provided little entertainment value, endless hours of news that caused even more stress, and entirely too much social media? Would you like a do-over? I sure would! Are there precious moments you wish you could get back? What are you glad that you did? What do you wish you had done? Perhaps more importantly, what do you wish you hadn't done?

What do you wish you had written?

I challenge you to take another look at that glass in light of the regrets, the "shoulda, woulda, couldas." With fresh eyes and renewed hope, consider the time you might have now that you did not consider before. Perhaps it is time saved getting ready for work in the morning or perhaps commuting to work because you now work from home; perhaps it is time saved by shopping online. Can you find 15-20 minutes per day or even an hour you didn't used to have? Identify that time, set it aside, guard it, and write, write, write. We have been given a good gift. God's gift of time.

Dear writers, be very careful, then, how you live—not as unwise but as wise, making the most of every opportunity. Remember, there is an occasion for everything, and a time for every activity under heaven. The time for the activity of writing is right now. *Carpe diem!*

Procrastination ... A Discourse

Derick Carstens

Let it be understood that this author suffers from chronic procrastination. It is an insidious and often delightful foe. Insidious because of its beguiling nature, alluring me to any other task save for the one at hand. Tempting me with the most earnest of television shows. Or the ever-important cleaning of the doom/junk drawer that hasn't been cleaned in seven years but suddenly must be cleaned this very moment. Moreover, how can I neglect the phone call to my high school best friend whom I haven't spoken with in the better part of two decades?

Procrastination is a master of disguise and comes in any form. There is a skill of routing it out and casting it into obscurity. Its name is routine—setting out to do a thing every day at the same time for the same duration. While not a perfect foil to the plans of procrastination, this will keep the beast at bay for a time.

The other thing that keeps the beast in its cage is passion. While this isn't a discipline that can be learned, it is one that can be fed. Set your routine around doing the thing you're most passionate about and allow yourself to fall completely in love with it. For our purposes, it's writing. Set a time and a day. Surround yourself with inspiration. Gather your favorite tools whether that is pen and paper or antique typewriter or the infinitely customizable electronic options.

Settle in and allow yourself to explore your creativity. Always keep in mind this is the thing you love, the thing that gives you life. Try not to lose that focus and the war with procrastination will be easier to win.

This short essay was written a day and a half before the submission deadline. Did I have months and months to complete it? Yes. Did I come up with the premise for it two months ago? Also yes.

I am writing to you as one who struggles with procrastination. I am actively putting in the work to do better. With the Lord's help and wisdom, this too will be a redeemed habit. My desire is to offer you hope and a little levity. Just because you haven't doesn't mean you won't. Set yourself before the Lord; remind yourself this is what you live to do. Be prepared for the awesomeness that will exude from you onto the page.

Write on, fellow writer, right on!

Next Time

DM Frech

It's been years since I saw my dad. He and my mom stood on their front porch and waved goodbye. It was a nice moment, and I thought I should take a picture. But, being busy, I told myself I would take their picture next time.

A day later my dad had a stroke and was no longer himself, yet he knew me. At the hospital he'd grab my hand every few seconds and say, "Debra, don't go, you're my ride home." Seconds later, "Debra, don't go, you're my ride home." This went on and on, and I was helpless to assure him. His brain never recovered, and he died a month later.

That last wave was the last time I saw my dad before his brain got blotted out. He was kind, funny, thoughtful, caring, had a great memory, and was always there to listen to everyone, even strangers. A good guy, he was the foundation on which our family stood, the glue that held together all the broken pieces. Without him, we fell apart.

Would my life have changed had I taken that last picture instead of telling myself, "Next time"? Probably not. But I often think about those words—next time. Those words poke me with regret.

One day I realized that God never tells us, "Next time." And I need to stop poking myself because God says, "Don't worry." "Do not fear." "Only believe." "He who had ears to hear let him hear." "Peace I leave you."

God gives hope, strength, love, but never says, "Next time."

Questions for Guided Journaling

What do you find most difficult about writing? What keeps you from sitting down and putting pen to paper (or fingers to keyboard) every day?

Work hard so you can present yourself to God and receive His approval. Be a good worker, one who does not need to be ashamed and who correctly explains the word of truth.
2 Timothy 2:15 (NLT)

EXCELLENCE

Do you see a man who excels in his work?
He will stand before kings;
He will not stand before unknown men.
Proverbs 22:29 (NKJV)

"I am careful not to confuse excellence with perfection. Excellence, I can reach for. Perfection is God's business."

Michael J. Fox

Love Your Readers
Dylan West

Love Your Reader As You Love Yourself.

This phrase is tattooed under my left eyelid so I'll never forget it. With that image in mind, you won't either. But what does loving readers look like? It starts with thinking more about their enjoyment and less about my success.

"As you love yourself" makes me ask: what do I want from stories? After thirty years of thought, here's my list:
- Every page surprises me.
- The story is so well thought-out I forget it's not real.
- It gives me an experience I can't get for myself.
- It's unlike anything I've ever read before.

From this, I see I want novelty and immersion. But when Ecclesiastes says *there is nothing new under the sun*, how can I expect something novel from a novel? At a high level, every kind of story has been done. There are five or seven or thirty-six archetypes, depending on which internet oracle you ask.

But low-level details are different. They should venture far from the ruts prior authors have worn into their genres. A thousand books have shown me this is possible. I've read scenes that startled me out of my chair and some that startled the food out of me. Sentences that made me stop and gawk like I'd found a twelve-leaf clover. Phrases that tickled the quiet questions icicling my brain. If others can do this, so can I.

As for immersion, I got a faceful of it with *Jurassic Park*. Furnace-blasted by years of medical school, Michael Crichton's science details felt so real that thirteen-year-old me went hunting velociraptors in the woods. The eight years of writing and research fossilized into that story gave me the most thrilling twelve hours of my bookish childhood. Think of that—eight years of labor for one day of wonder. In fact, Crichton had published twenty books before that. He spent a third of his life becoming an author able to bring dinosaurs to life. That makes me feel loved.

Now I occupy the body of middle-aged Dylan, remapping constellations of freckles across my chest whenever a new one appears. And every day, I try to live up to the heroes who lured me to a writing desk. I sweep aside questions like, "How do I get more sales and reviews?" in favor of better questions like, "How do I give readers the same novelty and immersion that turned me into a reading junkie?"

And now you know what's tattooed under my right eyelid. You see, teenage-me didn't care about Michael Crichton's writing success. I just wanted the glee of running from disemboweling dinos. In the same way, I can't expect readers to care about my career. I'm not the point. My readers are.

I don't ask friends to buy my books to support me. Instead, I ask them to try my books and buy only if they want more. I'm a business, not a charity. If my stories don't create the kind of moments that send hands into wallets, then my books should not sell. Proverbs 22:29 says, *Do you see a man who excels in his work? He will stand before kings; He will not stand before unknown men.* (NKJV)

I drift through digital alleys where authors plaster their book links and beg for buyers. They shout into voids and grumble of systems rigged against the little guy, praying for algorithmic angels to fling them up the sales ranks. And while there is some truth in these complaints, they focus on the wrong thing.

Because as much as marketing matters, the product matters more. Can my hours of practice be measured in the thousands? Have I written a million words? Have I read a hundred authors in my genre?

Wherever authors go to stand before kings, I'm ready to publish a highway of books to get there. When critique partners roast me, I will revise and peek through splayed fingers at the next set of comments. If chapter one needs 103 rewrites and I wear out the backspace key, I'll swipe my wife's keyboard and keep working. Don't tell her. The white knuckles and held breath of a thirteen-year-old reader are worth it.

People don't gush to their friends about mediocre books. They reserve that for ones that were better than they had to be, built by authors who waded through rivers of red ink. I want to be that author and write those books. To preach the Gospel long after I'm dead. To be the reason some kid starts biking to the library every summer.

How about you? Wanna join me? I know a good tattoo artist if you need one.

A Writer's Prayer

DEAR GOD, if it would be Your will, I would like to be a writer—a good writer. May my writing draw people closer to you as a C.S. Lewis or J.R.R. Tolkein story would.

Guide and direct my steps as I lay this desire before You. I pray that my stories would be good enough to be published and for enough time to pursue publication. If You have other plans, please guide and direct me.

Thank You for Your grace and mercy, showing us how to live and write stories.

In Jesus' name, Amen.

John Reddel

Confessions of Captain Obvious
Pam Piccolo

I haven't felt a real passion for writing for some time now. No need to go into the particulars other than to say that I've been miserable without it.

And it hasn't been from lack of prompting. As this writers group can testify, the resources shared with us each month have been steadfast and stimulating. The ubiquitous writing exercises, diversity of speakers, plethora of opportunities, and sheer enthusiasm of our fearless leader have been more than enough to inspire.

So, as they might say in New Jersey, what gives?

Borrowing from my trusty dictionary, why haven't I been "filled with the urge or ability to do or feel something creative"? What more could I possibly need to "stimulate, motivate, cause, incline, persuade, encourage, influence, rouse, move, stir, spur, goad, energize, galvanize, incite, incentivize, inspirit, impel, animate, or fire the imagination"?

It wasn't until a friend started lending me books on a regular basis that something clicked: *I had stopped reading.*

There was a time when I'd read cereal boxes just to have the written word in front of me. I don't remember exactly how or when the decline started or even why, but I was enamored no longer.

What does love of reading have to do with our craft? At the risk of mimicking Captain Obvious, there's an essential, mutually beneficial link between reading and writing.

Literacy advocate Pam Allyn, entitled a recent article "Reading Is Like Breathing In; Writing Is Like Breathing Out." What a concept! Allyn explains:

> Absorbing the nuances and understandings of written language through reading, the literacy learners put it all to use when going to the page or screen. Conversely, writing is an essential skill for students of all ages. It allows students to make sense of—and communicate about—what they have read and the world around them. It helps students learn to express opinions, make effective arguments, persuade audiences, synthesize information, and so much more.

In his article, "What I Tell Students When They Say They Don't Like to Read," teacher Terry Heick shares:

[In school] I never got a chance to understand why I should read . . . I knew it was good for me, like flossing. But I didn't really understand why. Some readers may love the idea or process of reading, but really what they love are ideas. The way writers can create pictures in your head. The way reading quiets your mind and relaxes you. But actually reading is just the way to get to those things . . . a strategy. Reading can help you do anything: take apart an engine, design a bridge, become inspired, understand other people, fall in love, experience every emotion imaginable. Fear. Curiosity. Contentment. Annoyance. Awkwardness. Pride. Longing. Books help you understand, and understanding helps you grow . . . I'm a different person when I finish a book than when I started.

I'd say that rings true whether it's a book you're reading or writing.

In *On Writing: A Memoir of the Craft*, Stephen King explains why reading is so important for those who want to write.

If you want to be a writer, you must do two things above all others: read a lot and write a lot. There's no way around those two things that I'm aware of, no shortcut . . . I don't read in order to study the craft; I read because I like to read . . . yet there is a learning process going on . . .

The real importance of reading is that it creates an ease and intimacy with the process of writing . . . constant reading will pull you into a place where you can write eagerly and without self-consciousness. It also offers you a constantly growing knowledge of what has been done and what hasn't, what is trite and what is fresh, what works and what just lies there dying (or dead) on the page. The more you read, the less apt you are to make a fool of yourself with your pen or word processor.

As author Anne Lamott points out, the converse is also true.

> Writing makes you a better reader. One reads with a deeper appreciation and concentration, knowing now how hard writing is, especially how hard it is to make it look effortless. You begin to read with a writer's eyes. You focus in a new way. You study how someone portrays his or her version of things in a way that is new and bold and original.

How does all this relate to the Christian writer? Here's how Andrew Collins sees it in his article, *Experiencing Scripture as Poetry*.

> As a former pastor of mine once remarked, poets are "shepherds of words." They facilitate wonder and awe in the face of our miraculous existence; they lift the veil to let us see the reality of God's work in the world.
>
> If this is true of great poetry and prose, then it must be even more true of Scripture . . . This God-breathed collection of letters, songs, and historical accounts on which we stake our beliefs and lives isn't merely a theology textbook; it's poetry and literature of the highest order.

Collins concludes, "We need every generation to keep creating so we can see the old truths afresh."

With all this in mind, I find myself looking forward to my friend's impromptu book-of-the-week club, reading with a new appetite to get my own words down on paper. I hope you will too.

May reading in general, and reading Scripture as the Author of Life intends, inspire us as shepherds of words, to make Him known to the world.

When Good Is Not Good Enough

Jayne Ormerod

Good is "good enough" when it comes to many things in life. For example, when it comes to cleaning the house, good is good enough. A little dust behind the piano never killed anyone. (Although my Great Aunt Tillie would disagree.)

Good is good enough when it comes to parallel parking. A tire hitched on the sidewalk isn't going to hurt anyone, especially since you're only running into the store for one thing. (It's a truth universally acknowledged that no one can ever go into a store for only one thing. Am I right?)

This truism also applies when it comes to golf. A drive down the fairway might hook or slice, but if you avoid the water hazard, then that's good enough. (But good enough might not be "good enough" if there are alligators roaming the greens. Just sayin'.)

So good is good enough in many life events. However, good enough is *not* good enough when it comes to writing. Success in writing requires nothing short of excellence.

What is excellence, you ask? That is an excellent question. First let's clarify that it should not be confused with perfection. That's defined as "freedom from fault or defect." When applied to writing, a piece can be without a single spelling error, or grammar slipup, and formatted to industry standards. Thus deemed "perfect." But it may, or may not (probably not), achieve literary "excellence."

Excellence means greatness, the very best. It goes way, way, way beyond the mechanics. Excellence in storytelling must achieve the highest levels in all story elements: theme, setting, characters, tone, point of view, conflict, and plot. Phew. That's a lot of parts. And before your eyeballs roll back into your head, we are not going to talk about each individual segment here. There are plenty of books/online resources/classes or workshops that will help you "perfect" each element.

Instead, let's focus on how a writer achieves this overall status of excellence. First, we must understand the concept. "Excellence is the gradual result of always striving to be better." No, I did not just make that up. Props go to NBA coach Pat Riley. He may have been referring to efforts on the basketball court, but it equally applies to efforts in your writing. You must keep writing, and rewriting, and rewriting, and . . . well, you get the point. Hey, nobody said writing was going to be easy. But you're probably reading this to find out what steps you can take to achieve excellence in your written work.

There are three things that will help you do just that.

First, you must have an honest heart-to-heart with your IE (internal editor). Ask yourself, "Is this excellent?" Some IEs are nicer than others and will stroke your ego before pointing out your foibles. My IE, on the other hand, has a particularly nasty disposition and hates everything I write. But we've learned to live/work together over the years. (Don't tell her that she's usually right…her ego is big enough as it is!) So, after your slightly evil IE says, "Good, but not good enough," you return to your chair and do better.

Once your IE is satisfied, ask a trusted family member or friend to read your work. I can almost promise you they will say it's good. They might even go so far as to proclaim it GUUUUUDDD. That's what friends are for. But their opinions cannot always be trusted, 1) because they don't want to hurt your feelings, and 2) they don't want things to be awkward next time you're seated next to each at a wedding reception. But I guarantee they have a few helpful comments/insights. What do you do now? Crawl back into your writing chair and write harder.

When you've polished your prose until it shines, it's time to join a CG (critique group). This is the best way to solicit unbiased opinions from other writers. And guess what? These trusted opinions are free (music to a struggling writer's ears!) Keep in mind that, by definition, their job is to find fault, and it's always nice when it's mixed with praise. Yes, sometimes the critiques hurt, but once the wound-licking is over you will find many helpful insights. Your work is not done, so back to the bat cave, Batman. (Oops . . . my age may be showing there.)

Lather, rinse, repeat until you achieve the elusive label of Literary Excellence. But how will you know when you've achieved excellence? Why, when the rave reviews . . . and massive royalties . . . start rolling in, of course.

Until then, keep writing. Keep believing. Keep striving for excellence. And never ever settle for "good enough."

Three Thoughts on Excellent Writing

Karen McSpadden

What makes a writer *excellent?* We look to everything from bestseller lists to international awards to dense literary journals as measures of excellent writing. But can *anyone* be excellent? Is it reserved for the Truly Big Deal authors, the once-in-a-generation lightning bolts? Is it for the wildly popular authors whose books fly off shelves and onto the movie screen and, I imagine, right into a hefty bank account? Or is there some aspect of excellence that every writer can—and *should*—reach for in their own writing practice, however humble? Did I mention that rhetorical questions are also a tool of excellent writing?

I propose that the pursuit of excellence is open to everyone who has ever picked up a pen, even to write a grocery list. I myself have written one or two truly excellent grocery lists. But I digress. Whoever you are, wherever you are in your writing journey, here are three thoughts to get you started:

Excellent writers show up for their writing work. I don't just mean sitting down to write. I mean the kind of "showing up" you do for your marriage, for your kids, even for your dog. For the stuff that matters. You give your time, your mind, your heart, all of it. No one else can do this part for you. No matter who else believes in you or encourages you, you're the only one who can show up for your writing day in and day out.

Excellent writers dream and learn. Who is the author you most admire? What do you love about them? What can you learn from them? How can they help you as you work on your own writing? Never stop dreaming . . . or learning. Curiosity killed the cat, but it keeps us writers alive.

Excellent writers are humble but stubborn. Of course, your first drafts—and maybe even your fifth drafts—might be horse manure. Recognize your limits. Embrace every single opportunity to grow and improve. But when it comes to believing that your ideas matter and that you are the one meant to explore those ideas, be a little stubborn. Be very stubborn. Don't let criticism, doubt, or temporary failure change that core belief. Grow your skill but keep your roots deep in what is true about your creative calling.

The pursuit of excellence is for all of us. And the best news is . . . you can get started *today.*

How important is excellence to you? Do you rewrite each manuscript until it is your very best work with no wasted words or weak phrases?

*Patient endurance is what you need now, so you will continue to do God's will.
Then you will receive all that He has promised.*
Hebrews 10:36 (NLT)

PRAYER

For this reason I am telling you, whatever things you ask for in prayer [in accordance with God's will], believe [with confident trust] that you have received them, and they will be given to you.

Mark 11:24 (AMP)

"You say grace before meals.
All right.
But I say grace before
the play and the opera,
and grace before
the concert and the pantomime,
and grace before I open a book,
and grace before
sketching, painting,
swimming, fencing, boxing,
walking, playing dancing;
and grace before
I dip the pen in the ink."

G.K. Chesterton

As You Write

As you write for God
And sometimes feel disheartened
Due to goals not met
Words hard pressed to grace the page
Time needed for other things
Be blessed by God's comfort

Stop and listen
He will tell you what to do
Be open to His suggestions
Get intimate with Him
Follow what He says
When all is lost, He finds a way
Write wherever and whenever you can
Whatever works, do it!

*Well then, does God supply you with the
Spirit and work miracles among you
by your doing the works of the law,
or by you believing what you heard?*
Galatians 3:5 (NRSV)

For that is your goal
To begin and to end
Delve into yourself
Pulling out what others need to see and hear
Knowing the benefits
For you have already received them

In my distress I called to the Lord
I cried to my God for help
From His temple he heard my voice,
My cry came before him, into His ears.
Psalm 18:6 (NIV)

Always know,
you can call on the Lord.

Mary Stasko

A Writer's Prayer

Father, Let me draw near to You and be still; to know Your voice and hear Your words. Words, not just for me but those around me.

Life is often dark and we become weary.
An encouraging word of love can find its way to a troubled world that yearns for light in the darkness.

May I be a funnel that You can pour through—not merely a container to be filled and just sit stagnant. May Your joy and glory be expressed in my words and in my very life.

In Jesus' name, Amen.

Kathy Daugherty

10 Different Places to Pray
Olivia Arney

1. The Swing
When I was a child, I talked like a child, I thought like a child, I reasoned like a child. When I became a man, I put the ways of childhood behind me. (1 Corinthians 13:11 NIV)

I pray here to remind me of my childhood. You might be surprised to think a playground swing would be an ideal place to cry out to Jesus during some of my most trying times. After not talking to my Lord and Savior for quite some time and my heart is pulling, tugging to get away from utter darkness, a reminder of the innocence is my sanctuary. There's nothing like sitting on the U-shaped seat, holding the chains as I swish my legs on the mulch, and beginning a conversation with Him. On a beautiful day, whether it be my own backyard or at the park down the street, it's like we pick up right where we left off.

2. The Corner
Let us then approach God's throne of grace with confidence, so that we may receive mercy and find grace to help us in our time of need. (Hebrews 4:16 NIV)

The corner? The corner of what exactly? The corner of anything. A bedroom or living room, preferably somewhere in the house. Face the wall or lean against it if you need to. Close your eyes or leave them open. Think of anything that reminds you of Jesus. Use those reminders to get back to your state of prayer. This can help you be present in the moment.

3. While Running/Walking
Ask and it will be given to you; seek and you will find; knock and the door will be opened to you. For everyone who asks receives; the one who seeks finds; and to the one who knocks, the door will be opened. (Matthew 7:7-8 NIV)

Running/walking requires you to go from one place to another and is representative of our journey with Christ. We are supposed to run to God and run away from the evils of this world. Pray while exercising on the treadmill or venturing on outdoor trails. Use that time to thank the Lord for your everyday blessings or to ask Him about anything else during the rumble-jumble in a busy day.

4. The Car
He will call on me, and I will answer him; I will be with him in trouble, I will deliver him and honor him. With long life I will satisfy him and show him my salvation. (Psalm 91:15-16 NIV)

You may be thinking that praying while driving would be too much of a distraction—or that it might be a good idea when you're trying to prevent road rage against someone that cut you off. Praying is not the same as a phone call. Think of using the car as a base to pray about other things. Sometimes I'm just sitting behind the wheel, completely still and parked, because I don't want to get out. I've had those days. Those days where I feel stuck. Where I feel trapped. A long drive, or even a short one, gives me plenty of time to think about the things I want to say to the Lord.

5. School
Therefore confess your sins to each other and pray for each other so that you may be healed. The prayer of a righteous person is powerful and effective. (James 5:16 NIV)

If you're not in school anymore, this can apply to your workplace, too. As a college student, school as a place to pray resonates with me. Maybe you need to pray for a coworker who is annoying the heck out of you. I know I need to check myself with the way I'm treating or thinking about a classmate that may have done me wrong in some way but may not have even realized it.

6. The Garden
Then Jesus went with his disciples to a place called Gethsemane, and he said to them, "Sit here while I go over there and pray." (Matthew 26:36 NIV)

What garden? Certainly not the Garden of Eden! It could be the garden in your backyard or perhaps the botanical gardens. If you don't have a garden, maybe you know someone who does. What better way to worship God than to admire nature. The colorful flowers sprouting up from the soil and the abundant vegetable plants from God's powerful creation strike inspiration at any given moment.

7. While Traveling
And pray in the Spirit on all occasions with all kinds of prayers and requests. With this in mind, be alert and always keep on praying for all the Lord's people. (Ephesians 6:18 NIV)

Traveling doesn't necessarily mean vacation. It could be way less fun—like a business trip. While I've been on little trips in the past with family, I find myself around people I've either never met or rarely see. The opportunity presents itself to tell the truth and be kind to whoever you're with in the unfamiliar environment.

8. The Water
Whoever believes in me, as Scripture has said, rivers of living water will flow from within them. (John 7:38 NIV)

Living near the beach my whole life, I've had many intense connections to the Holy Spirit while floating on my back and looking up at the sky. Walking along the shore, I compare the crashing waves or the rough sand to the hardships of life. A boat ride can bring a similar experience. I've kayaked, canoed, and paddle boarded, and can say there's something about the gliding feeling that brings ease to the soul.

9. The Store
Therefore, I tell you, whatever you ask for in prayer, believe that you have received it, and it will be yours. And when you stand praying, if you hold anything against anyone, forgive them, so that your Father in heaven may forgive you your sins. (Mark 11: 24-25 NIV)

I've found myself saying little prayers when I'm out shopping. Not just about the products I'm buying (although I do that too), but other random things. I'm not a big spender so perhaps the rustle-tussle of shops overwhelms me. I get distracted—in a good way. Prayer draws me to God instead of worldly things.

10. The Tree
The fruit of the righteous is a tree of life, and the one who is wise saves lives. (Proverbs 11:30 NIV)

This also connects back to my childhood, although I firmly believe you are never too old to climb a tree. Two giant magnolias live in our front yard. I could climb to the top of one and see the whole neighborhood—rooftops and five backyards—like a helicopter view labeled the "whole neighborhood" in my head. I feel a great deal of peace—hardly nervous at all—sitting on the branches nearly 50 feet high. Now the getting down part—I might need to say a little prayer about that.

Reflection: Prayer, though beautiful, is difficult for some people. I'm one of those people. That's the reason this is not an instructional guide. I'm not telling anyone how to pray. I'm merely sharing my suggestions and my own experiences. I admire Christians that can pray to God throughout their whole day in all their little actions and before every decision they make. It's like they never stop talking in an ongoing conversation with God. Prayer is about building our relationship with Him. I've attempted this before, and it hasn't worked out the way I'd like. But I won't stop trying. I remind myself that prayer isn't about things going my way or how I'd like something to be. It's about honoring Him.

As a writer, prayer journals are often a way to express the important words in your mind. The amazing thing is that you can look back on your prayers and their answers and see what God has done.

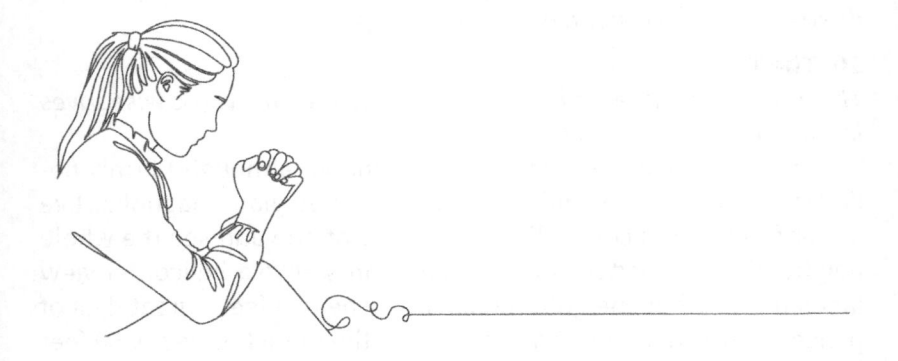

A Writer's Work

You are not a nerd
Letting your thoughts go skyward
Asking God for help along the way
Continuing the flow, say
Whatever comes from your heart
Press on from the start
Get into a routine so then
Every day you begin again
Writing what matters most

Asking God for His Blessing
The design from Him woven in on a wing
Keeping true
A light in view
For once complete
Then edit and check before you beat
It down and re-write
Your craft with continued insight
Seek out others for more to delight

More changes, corrections, sense
Continuity hence
The final work complete
Submit now with intent and heat
Moving to publish and sell
Your work to those who will wish you well.

Mary Stasko

A Writer's Prayer

Lord, I am struggling to pray. It's difficult to express what's on my mind, though my heart always knows what needs to be said. I am thankful that You know me even more than I know myself.

Please bless me with patience when I strain to find the words to put on paper. Regardless of how I feel, help me be a strong shoulder of support for those who likewise struggle. Give me the words to inspire and build up and never tear down. May this also include the words that I say to myself. Sometimes terrible mantras like to take a spin in my mind, and their harmful effects taunt me for days.

Help me reflect on Your love when I'm at my worst, not just when I'm at my best. May I be honest in my words and worry less about what others may think. Give me the gentle reassurance that my words still matter, even if the only eyes to see my work are my own. That there is a beauty in delving deep within, perhaps even carving the words out of my soul. That those words deserve to be written, deserve to be said.

Thank You for the days when I'm at my peak, contentment swimming through my veins as words pour out of me like an abundant waterfall. I am forever grateful that, in this sea of people, You took a moment to give me a love for words and the heart of a storyteller. May I not waste what I've been given.

Please continue to give us all encouragement and peace in our writing. May every word written bring a sense of renewal and fulfillment in who we are as artists, as curators of words and thoughts summed up on a page. May we look to You for confidence as we move forward, taking it one word at time, page upon page, whether short or long. May we look to you for reassurance in who we are, hoping that our doubts may be short-lived, and for grace and guidance—the most important request of all.

Thank You, Lord, for all You have done and all You will do.

In Jesus' name, Amen.

Lori Higgins

Questions for Guided Journaling

Regarding your writing, what priority do you give prayer?

_____
_____
_____
_____
_____
_____
_____
_____
_____
_____
_____

*Devote yourselves to prayer
with an alert mind and a thankful heart.*
Colossians 4:2 (NLT)

QUESTIONS FOR GUIDED JOURNALING: BONUS PAGE!

Take a few minutes and write your own prayer.

_____
_____
_____
_____
_____
_____
_____
_____
_____
_____
_____
_____
_____
_____
_____

"Thus speaks the Lord God of Israel, saying: 'Write in a book for yourself all the words that I have spoken to you.'"
Jeremiah 30:2 (NKJV)

The Writer's Psalm

Praise to the One who has withheld nothing. Glory to the One whose love we are bound up in. All honor to the One whose grace is beyond human.

Daddy, I enter the throne room and climb up into Your lap and recline in Your extravagant love. How grateful I am that You know my voice and every hair on my head. You dry my tears, sing and dance over me . . . You've prepared a place for me, and Your thoughts of me outnumber the grains of sand.

How simply miraculous is Your sovereign love.

No one has ever spoken for me like You have.
No one has ever loved me like You, and no one has been able to change me from the inside out like You're doing.
Thank you, Father, for Your hand is open to me and Your face shines upon me.

I request of Your generous heart a fresh vision of the instrument I am in Your hands. Show Your servant how I am "able to do greater things than these," as You proclaimed I would.

May my pen bring You fame.

Use it to provide life-giving words of encouragement at just the right moment to those who are spiritually on their hands and knees struggling to move forward.

May it change hearts and lives of those who no longer have hope. Let it be the lifeline for those who feel worthless. Allow it to be living water to cracked, dry souls. Use it to share Your heart and touch those who are barely standing.

As a child of Abraham, I offer up my teachable heart and ask for the ability to set the page for a God encounter. May it be said, "How beautiful is the pen of the one who brings the good news of Christ."

Messiah, encourage Your servant today. Set my soul on fire. Let my pen be the flame that burns as bright as the mere twelve who, through their obedient, sold-out, won-over hearts, dug the roots of Christianity. Empower us to build upon their foundation.

Yahweh, no one within my grasp should perish without the knowledge of Your love for them. Everyone deserves to be loved, Ho see their value through Your eyes.
Love has a voice—Jesus.
Love has a name—Jesus.

Jehovah, give me a double dose of courage like that of David or Esther, to go where You're leading. The kind of courage that would cause me to lift a pen filled with gratitude and extend a helping hand, all because of what You have done for me.

Thank You, Daddy, that You do not remember me according to my transgressions, but rather You remember me according to Your great love for me.

In my heart, I believe I have asked according to Your will. Therefore, in the name of the precious Lamb Jesus, I thank You.

Sherrie Pilkington

"Your talent is God's gift to you.
What you do with it
is your gift back to God."
Leo Buscaglia

Photography by DM Frech

Try Your Hand

*Oh, magnify the L*ORD *with me,
and let us exalt His name together.
I sought the L*ORD *and He heard me,
and delivered me from all my fears.*
Psalm 34:3-4 (NKJV)

Writing Prompts

Evelyn J. Wagoner

If you have ever perused a brick-and-mortar or digital bookshelf looking for books on writing, you've doubtless run across multiple volumes dedicated to writing prompts. There's good reason for this.

Want to improve your writing? Write! Prompts are great if you're trying to develop consistency in your daily writing, are fighting writer's block, or just want to turn the writing faucet on.

Every month during our group meeting, we participate in a writing exercise to get the juices flowing. It's simple. The prompt is read aloud, and everyone writes like crazy for five minutes.

There are only three rules:

1. Don't second guess yourself—go with the first thought that pops into your head. If you think, "Surely, I can come up with something better than that," you'll use up the entire five minutes.

2. Get your pen moving right away and keep writing until you come to a conclusion you're happy with or the clock runs out.

3. Don't edit unless you have time at the end. This is pretty much stream-of-consciousness writing.

It's amazing how an entire room of writers can work from the same prompt and each come up with something entirely unique. We're including some samples of our exercises. Some are five-minute creations and others are a bit longer, as we also assign a prompt to work on during the month.

Go ahead. Try your hand! What comes immediately to mind when you read the prompt? After all, writers write!

Writing Exercise
Jennifer Napier
Prompt: *They're talking in whispers*

I'm Choosing Life

No one likes to speak loudly when the unthinkable happens.
The tragedy of a 21-year-old, beautiful young woman who is almost eight months pregnant
should not be able to die.
But she did.
And just like that she was taken.
In a moment, in a heartbeat ... gone.
No more breaths. No more laughs. No more tears.
No comparing stretch marks.
No discussing parenting methods over desperate cups of coffee.
No more books to share or words to exchange.
No more helping me and supporting me through the trials of this life.
No more new shoes and shopping trips.
No more arched eyebrows or gasps of surprise with hands on hips.
No more hearing her voice lifted up in worship.
No more, no more, no more.
It's been 20 years and they stopped their whispers a long time ago.
They hang back and there's a subtle discomfort as they
remember the day where she tragically left this world.
When my earth stopped spinning and theirs went on without her.
Time heals all wounds they say ... no, it doesn't. It changes them.
And you can choose...
You can choose to grow.
You can choose to find gratitude.
You can choose to fight for joy.
Or you can become bitter,
Heartbroken that leaves you cold and dead inside.
I'm choosing life.
Choosing to honor her by living life to the full.
Enjoying God's good gifts ... and knowing it won't be long
til I breathe my last
and walk into that room.

Writing Exercise
Paula Grimsley
Prompt: *They spoke in whispers*

Secret Thoughts

Fearing to be overheard, they spoke in whispers. The invading rebels could not overhear their strategy if whispered! Since a large part of the world's population disappeared, including women and children, they had to move around stealthfully. Only during times of darkness when their path was shrouded in night's blackness.

What happened? Why did all the people disappear?

Cars left without drivers, crumpled clothing on the seats of airplanes and buses. What could've happened, they whispered their secret thoughts. A takeover by the undercover police?

How would he get a message to Mohammed their newest recruit?

Every telephone message had the potential to be intercepted. They had to speak in whispers, so as not to be overheard!

Suddenly the crunching of leaves. Eerie footsteps approached them in their hiding space. Try not to breathe, he whispered.

Writing Exercise
Ann Abraham
Prompt: *Write about a gate.*

The Garden Gate
Picture of a fallow past / ode to a hopeful future

The young girl hesitated a moment before opening the sliding patio door. Looking back into the family room filled with boxes, furniture piled up, and fragile items covered with bubble wrap, she knew this was her last chance. It would be her final voyage into the realm she had cherished for the most important and precious years of her life.

Wise beyond her twelve years, she had a sense that drinking in the view of her backyard one last time was vital. More important though—the garden beckoned. The green escape was always a welcome spot when things got too much to bear inside the house. Sometimes fragrant, sometimes fallow, depending upon her mother's mood or the growing season, the rows of long-dead corn stalks and overgrown tomato stakes hid her from view.

Her mother was too busy with the baby to miss her when she stepped out that back door, and she could take a book and read for hours, living a life of romantic ease or following the trail of a haunting mystery, depending upon the whim of the author. Beyond view of prying eyes, this was her chance to bury her worries behind her childhood home's garden gate, and she planned to make the most of this last hour before the move.

The future seemed bleak when she had first stepped out the back door, but she was smiling as she reached out her hand to open the gate to the garden, book in hand.

Writing Exercise
Rachel Plumley
Prompt: *We stopped walking in the woods.*

Get Back Up

Summer of 2013 is drenched in green. We live in the Emerald State, Seattle, Washington. I pile three boys in my Jeep: a first-grader, toddler, and baby. Our own urban oasis, a short drive from home, Schmitz Park is tucked away like the giant stone troll under a bridge. It doesn't look like much when you parallel park against the curb. A yellowed trail guide is tacked behind plexiglass. But ten steps down the trail, the city is no more.

Boys march in matching rain boots. They drop Buzz Lightyear backpack and sippy cups in favor of mossy stick swords. Giant spruces bow, a canopy across our path. We stop walking to say hello to the alligator-painted redwood. We stopped a moment too long. The toddler is gone and the youngest baby is tottering toward a drop off! My one remaining boy, the eldest, the responsible one, looks left and I run right. I scoop up baby just before he careens off the edge. I hear Bradley announce that he's tracking either Pooh bear sniffling through the forest or he's found his brother.

We're finally together again. I will my anxiety to melt away as we dip toes in a happy stream. A nurse log is fallen across the stream, home to a whole tiny ecosystem. She is dead but her decomposing body hosts ferns, flowers, insects, and new baby trees. While I nourish these babies with my body, mother's milk, weary arms, heart aching when they run away, I must take care to get back up when I fall.

Writing Exercise
Olivia Arney
Prompt: *Write about spring cleaning.*

The Most Important Person

Yardwork. Organizing the closet. Cleaning out the bathroom. Rearranging your bedrooms and the kitchen. Oftentimes, these phrases can be associated with the term *spring cleaning*. But what about cleaning our souls? I promise I'm not trying to get all existential on you by asking that question. It's just something to consider. After all, Easter is celebrated in the spring.

When Jesus came to visit Mary and Martha in their home, Jesus noticed Martha was only worried about getting the chores done, while Mary paid her full attention to the most important Person in the room. This is a reminder that we ought to cleanse our spirits. If we have a messy heart, we may distract ourselves with cleaning. That doesn't mean we shouldn't keep our houses clean. This is not intended as an accusation of people acting more like a Martha when they should be a Mary, but we're all guilty of shortcomings. Let's purify ourselves physically and spiritually.

In all thy ways acknowledge Him, and He shall direct thy paths. (Proverbs 3:6 KJV)

Writing Exercise
Dylan West
Prompt: *Write about digging a hole.*

Lalibela

If your holy city is overtaken by Muslims, what should you do? Fight? Pray? Negotiate? How about digging out a series of new churches in solid stone? That's what Lalibela did in the late 1100s when Saladin took Jerusalem in 1187 AD.

We've all heard about the cathedrals of Europe—how master stonemasons quarried stone blocks, carted them to a building site, then stacked them cleverly into soaring shapes. (Think of a 3D printer.) But Lalibela? He did none of that. Instead, he chiseled out all the stone that didn't belong to form underground churches. Literal ones.

Each church was made of one solid stone. (Think of a CNC milling machine.) And he didn't carve one, but thirteen of them! Their walls and ceilings are decorated with carvings and frescoes. Many are still used for Christian Orthodox ceremonies today. Other monolithic churches exist, but only these have free-standing external walls—the others are more like cave monasteries.

1 Corinthians 10:31 says, *So, whether you eat or drink, or whatever you do, do all to the glory of God.* (ESV)

What did Lalibela do? He dug holes.

Writing Exercise
Lori Higgins
Prompt: *Write about what you (or a character) wanted to say but didn't.*

Silence of My Heart

I still remember the way her hand slid against mine, and the way her lips twisted before she averted her eyes. I should have told her then how much she meant to me, but I couldn't. There was a finality as I gripped the reins of my horse tighter, as she moved away to say goodbye to her father.

Our small world was about to change. Long gone were our childhood days of climbing trees or sitting in the lavender field as she made us crowns to wear. I always appeased her wish as she giggled when I proudly wore the fragrant crown, and now I prepare to ride for the King who has traded in his own for one of iron. For now, anyway.

She turns back to me and pulls the veil that I know covers her dark hair, hair I won't see again until the day we are wed. At least, I promise myself, I will be able to tell her then, the words I need to say, the ones I do not even know how to say. I do know that she will be on my mind every morning and night until my return from the Holy Land. For now, I lean into the wait and hope I will survive to see her again.

Writing Exercise
Pam Piccolo
Prompt: *Write about an inappropriate time to laugh.*

The Cleansing Power of an Inappropriate Laugh

I have only fond memories of my Nonna, Maria. A Jackie Kennedy acolyte, she dressed in pert, patterned shifts, with short, white gloves, suitably subtle makeup and jewelry, and handbags more like miniature luggage that clicked closed with a tap. Topping off the portrait was a snowy mountain of luxuriously thick, perfectly-coiffed hair, one of the few signs of aging beauty often attributed to the "good genes" of her Italian heritage. Whether on her way to the grocery store or a holiday gathering, this was her unwavering uniform of style and grace.

Not only did Nonna look the part, she was in many ways a genuine, "mid-century modern." Dedicated to healthy eating and often ahead of the trends, she put into practice all recommendations of *Prevention Magazine* to the betterment of her reluctant family. Used to the staples of pasta and vino, which in their opinion were legitimate food groups, some remained unconvinced of the merit of her efforts. But that never stopped her. Sidestepping conventional barriers, her doting included chauffeuring under-aged grandchildren to rock concerts du jour. She'd later be found engaged in parking-lot conversation with non-ticket-holding teenagers expressing gratitude for their newfound, albeit "ancient" friend by placing flowers in her hair. Her unconditional listening skills bridged the celebrated age gap few could understand, let alone span.

What really set her apart, though, was her singular devotion to optimism. There was beauty to be found in every beast and good under every circumstance, as evidenced by her favorite admonishment, "You can just as easily laugh as cry." To her, the Depression era occasioned block parties, where neighbors feasted on leftovers, swapped hand-me-downs, and shared burdens as well as dreams for the next generation. Lost jobs, financial woes, marital tensions, even wayward children were nothing a good laugh couldn't conquer.

Rather than dampen her enthusiasm, the hilarity of every senior moment gave opportunity to overcome the absurdities of life with the joy of her self-deprecating humor. Only the hindsight of a million lost causes magnified by a myriad of unmet expectations affords a proper appreciation of the cleansing power of an inappropriate laugh. Thanks to Nonna, I've not only inherited but have come to cherish this freeing perspective. As the Scriptures explain, "love hopes all things."

An Inappropriate Time to Laugh

1. During a 21-gun salute
2. When the officiant says, "If anyone can show just cause why this couple cannot lawfully be joined together in matrimony, let them speak now or forever hold their peace."
3. During the sentencing phase of a murder trial
4. When the conference speaker stutters
5. After rear-ending your neighbor's brand new Land Rover
6. In response to any and all questions asked by the police officer at the scene
7. During a moment of silence for lost loved ones
8. At grandma's untimely bodily function noises (unless she does)
9. After the visiting pastor's wife sings
10. When a patient disrobes for a medical exam
11. At a war memorial

12. When an acquaintance unexpectedly expresses his/her undying love
13. When your enemy gets what he/she deserves
14. When children cry
15. At the pain of others
16. During your boss's acceptance speech at an awards ceremony
17. At someone's misfortune
18. When children use offensive language
19. At your mother-in-law's bad hair day
20. At cruelty
21. At the sacrifice of others
22. At a child's innocent remark
23. At vulgar jokes
24. When being disciplined
25. When someone puts a gun to your head
26. Behind someone's back
27. At jokes based on stereotypes
28. At the embarrassment of others
29. At someone's hard work, ingenuity, or creativity
30. At someone's accent, appearance, or failures
31. When someone gets away with wrongdoing
32. When you should be repenting

Writing Exercise
Evelyn J. Wagoner
Prompt: *Write about a familiar smell.*

To All the Ships at Sea

I must have looked like a puppy, my head hanging out the backseat window, eyes closed in the icy wind. In absolute bliss, I filled my lungs with deep, intoxicating breaths of that wonderful aroma. Ah—there's nothing like the exhilarating scent of oil, creosote, steel, and only-God-and-the-U.S. Navy know what else.

A friend had taken us to see the holiday lights at the Naval Base—a treat I hadn't had since I was a girl. But it wasn't the hundreds of thousands of lights adorning the ships or the snow flurries or even the nostalgic Christmas music on the radio that prompted a sense of longing and something evocative but unidentifiable in my heart.

What is it? It wasn't the first time I'd tried to understand the lifelong allure of the curious scents so unique to a Navy base.

Suddenly a memory flashed—and it all clicked: my father holding a tiny me close in his arms; my face—in relief and little-girl love—pressed against his neck, his cheek, his uniform.

So that was it. It wasn't at all the perfume of steel ships and concrete piers that had mesmerized me ever since I was a little girl. It was the fragrance of a daddy coming home.

Writing Exercise
Ann Abraham
Prompt: *Write about a signpost.*

Signposts of the Times

Mom warned me things would be different the next time I go back to Indiana to visit.

"You'll need to go down to Hoosier Road and see all the changes."

Since my parents moved even farther out of Indy to escape developers—away from Hoosier Road in Hamilton County to what I like to tease them is "beyond the middle of nowhere" an hour away—the farm on the tiny plot of land where I had grown up in Fishers had disappeared, tilled under, and re-created as a suburban development.

Rather than spend a fortune on a plane ticket or 14 hours on the road, I decided to check out the changes via Google Earth. Even using the Internet, it was odd turning off at the sign for Exit 5 Corporate Parkway—the uninventive name that had lazily become the small city's name for the area I used to call home. Passing Cumberland Road, seeing signs for new housing developments on land where I rode horses with my friends on their farms or had hunted in the woods, I felt a queasy feeling in the pit of my stomach. Time had turned over, and I was now on the wrong side of this sickening commercialized alternate reality.

Farther down 116th Street, I passed what used to be the Klotz' farm, now a large subdivision named Spyglass Falls. I doubled back to the entrance when I noticed the name of the street—Klotz Farm Blvd—and thought warmly of sitting in "Grandma" Klotz's kitchen before we went sledding down the one slope tall enough to make it possible in Hamilton County. How appropriate that the Klotz family got some recognition since they were some of the last holdouts among those farmers fighting the developers so many years ago.

Sadly, the Gouwens's farm had no similar commemoration, and, where the entrance to my friend Beth's house once stood, there was now a sign for Sand Creek Woods. I thought of the two-story green house and the large red barn with the horses and the smell of hay and horse dung. (Funny, while that is a smell I always associated with that house, along with the cigarette smoke from her dad's chain-smoking habit, somehow, it's not a bad memory.)

Up ahead, I saw the intersection I was looking for and, though it was now a spruced-up, four-lane intersection with traffic lights instead of a stop-or-you-might-miss-it country road, Hoosier Road was about what I expected with the borrow pit (now Lake Stonebridge) on the right and a large field with a white fence on the opposite corner.

The large dairy farm on the left that was surrounded by that fence, (I wondered if it was still owned by the Allen family), with its many barns and silos, stood in stark contrast to the suburban sprawl that had taken over the little corner of Fishers I had called home. Mom had always used this corner, with its pretty white fencerow and cows in the field, to give our friends directions to our farm—and it felt right that this neatly painted fence and picture-perfect farm still existed next to the new, upscale homes and organized streets (even if the cows were hidden from view).

By this point, my stomach was settled and I was ready—or thought I was ready—for the next sight.

Passing 121st Street, a brand-new elementary school now took the place of the large field that had always been on the side of our farm. A subdivision snaked its way behind and around and, where my driveway used to be, there was now a nicely manicured two-lane divided entrance to "Sumerlin Trails." (Why on earth would they have named it that? There should be some kind of tribute to our family heritage or name, or even the families who lived there before us. The tiny farmhouse we used to call home had a 150-year history. Somehow, it felt like there should have been some link to the past, at least a mention of the church that used to meet in the historic house.)

I tried to find familiar landmarks, but every vestige of our farm was gone. There had been a very tall, old-growth fir tree that stood right at the front of our house. Gone. Even the tall microwave tower next to the lake was gone, and I remembered how it had once so prominently overshadowed our little corner of Hamilton County. The road itself was different. What was once a rutted, barely two-lane asphalt road was now paved with turn lanes, making everything much easier to traverse than when I got the VW Dasher stuck in the ditch as a pre-teen.

After looking around a bit more, down Olio Road and past the old high school where so many of my friends wrecked their cars while learning to drive, and then backtracking again to 121st Street where the Smith's farm was now another development and the old mechanic's junkyard ceased to exist, I expanded my view of the area to look from above. Only a few farms remained in the surrounding acreage, now replaced by the commercial realities of fast-food restaurants, retail stores, and even what mom says the older locals call the "monstrosity" of a Top Golf.

I have a clearer picture now, almost 30 years later, why my parents—and the Klotzes, and Gouwens for that matter—all decided to give in to the developers and relocate to pastures farther away. The nostalgia of today's "Google" trip down memory lane, with all the signposts along the way, helped me understand their desire to move on to their new farms "beyond the middle of nowhere."

For now, my mom can still enjoy giving friends directions to their new farm based on the "crooked tree at the corner, the pond at the curve in the road, and the cows in the field"—until the day when the developers come calling again and the cycle begins anew. When I go back for my next visit, I'll do my best to appreciate those familiar signposts of farm life and pay respect to the humble farmers represented along the way.

No one remembers the former generations, and even those yet to come will not be remembered by those who follow them. (Ecclesiastes 1:11 NIV)

Writing Exercise
Dylan West
Prompt: *Write about fog (include a metaphor).*

Fog

    Fog rose from the pores of the earth whenever a momentous occasion drew near. I learned to squint through the mist for the outlines of an oncoming tragedy or delight, as they came without fail within a few days' shadow.

    The fog itself never caused the event as far as I could discern, but shrouded the event from fretful eyes, and I'm the only mortal who seems to notice this. Others think me mad, but I know what I'm seeing. As I write this, my windows are clouding over, and I wonder what it means for the launch of my newest enterprise.

Writing Exercise
Patti Jarrett
Prompt: *Write about finding something unusual at a yard sale.*

Dumpster Diva

The Marines are on the move—it's transfer time. A plethora of packing and purging permeates the hilltop apartment complex near Quantico. The heroine of our story, who shall remain anonymous, dashes to the corner of the parking lot and dives into a nearby—no, it's not a phone booth, but a trash receptacle—and out comes Dumpster Diva. It's the no-sale rummage sale. It's the yard sale with neither price tags, negotiations, nor a yard. It's true, one man's trash is another man's new wardrobe! On one occasion, DD rescued jeans in her size—and found $20 in the pocket, to boot.

Writing Exercise
Pam Piccolo
Prompt: *We stopped walking in the woods that summer.*

The Fall of Man

No walking in the woods that day
Outcast, filled with regret
Choice brought them fatal consequence
Predictions left unmet

He'd planted every tree therein
A garden to be sure
Two trees stood out with different fruit
One deadly, one the cure

Today we live with their mistake
On this we can agree
No matter how they tried
They missed the forest for the tree

Thank God one tree was left for us
On which we can rely
On Calvary's cross the Savior hung
For us He came to die

There'll be another tree someday
With healing for mankind
Its fruit will give eternal life
God's plan before all time

Writing Exercise
Joyce Hammer
Prompt: *Write about seeing someone for the last time.*

The Last Time I Saw Her

She was sitting at the kitchen table snapping beans fresh from our garden for supper. For as long as I could remember, Mom and Dad had planted a garden. She, and her dad before her, loved gardening and enjoyed harvesting fresh vegetables.

I had just dropped by my parents' house to get a few of my belongings. Bob and I had returned the night before from our honeymoon, and I came to transfer my belongings to our new house. I raced upstairs, grabbed some clothes and a few other items, and threw them in a bag.

As I came downstairs, I paused for a moment, wondering, "Should I sit down and snap beans with Mom for a few minutes?" I chose not to stop but to hurry to my new home.

It was a decision I lived to regret.

That was the last time I saw her. The following day she had a massive heart attack and died. It's worth taking a little extra time for people you love.

Writing Exercise
DM Frech
Prompt: *Write about rain.*

Rain

Rain is lovely, unless you're wearing silk and you're outside. Or you're in the middle of a golf game, or you're cutting grass, or camping, or there's so much rain lakes form around your house, or you're in the woods hiking and the trail becomes a series of tiny waterfalls.

I love rain, just like I love dogs, unless they're growling or barking at me, or horses unless they're trying to buck me off. I love nature unless it's poison ivy. Or a rattlesnake. I love long walks on the beach except when it rains. Okay, back to rain.

In the Old Testament, there was time God used rain for great destruction. Rain is powerful. I always wondered why God used rain to teach mankind a lesson. He flooded the earth and in doing so destroyed much of what He had created to start over.

Sometimes, starting over is necessary and, on that note, I segue to starting over. Rain has that quality. After a downpour, it feels like the earth starts over, unless it causes a river to flood that you accidentally fall into and are in danger of drowning.

Writing Exercise
Patti Jarrett
Prompt: *Write about a holiday fiasco.*

The Holiday Fiasco

'Twas the night before Christmas when we arrived, with a truckload of toys that made Santa's sleigh look like a Mini Cooper.

"Minnie Cooper? Wasn't she a rock star back in the 1900s?"

"No, Mom. That was Alice. Alice Cooper. And he was a guy."

"Oh," she replied, as she turned to go back into the house. "It was so hard to tell the girls from the fellas back then."

Following her into the house, I said, "We have a carload of presents to put under your tree, uh, where is your Christmas tree? I thought you put it up before Thanksgiving this year."

"I did put it up before Thanksgiving, but I took it down when the holidays were over."

"Kevin and I will get it from the garage, put it up, and then we'll bring the presents in."

"It's not in the garage, dear. After the holidays, I gave it to Jim, next door, to burn in his fireplace."

"Mom, it was an artificial tree!"

"Well, he's got an artificial fireplace. It looks like a fireplace, but you can't fool me. I know what a real fireplace looks like. I used to hang my stockings to dry above one, after I milked the cows. Santa came one night and put oranges in my stockings! I declare, they never did fit right after that."

Kevin and I debated whether to try to find a tree lot that night, or pay Jim a visit to see if he had Mom's. In the meantime, she dozed off in her recliner, visions of sugarplums dancing in her head.

Writing Exercise
Dylan West
Prompt: *We stopped walking in the woods that summer.*

Walking in the Woods

We stopped walking in the woods that summer when we came across a hole that seemed bottomless. I dropped a rock into it and never heard it clatter. We shined the strongest flashlight we had and found darkness beyond our light beam. Then my friend flew her high-powered quad copter camera drone into it. She needs it for her real estate photos, so I was worried, but she insisted. The camera gave us live footage of the hole as it descended, the lens pointing straight down into the black. It descended about 50 meters before we got a warning that it was approaching its max control range, so my friend started pulling up. Or tried to. The copter ignored her controls and kept gliding down.

Over the next few hours, we watched the soil turn to rock, and the rock change from gray to black, from black to bright red, then back to black and gray again. How we kept signal and how the battery lasted so long is beyond my understanding.

Finally, the gray rock turned to soil and the camera's view broke free into a sky that was bright blue and wide open. As the camera panned around, we saw a big yellow ball in the sky and white puffs floating around it.

We'd heard stories of such a place, but nobody actually believed it was real.

Writing Exercise
Pam Piccolo
Prompt: *If your life were a movie, write about the soundtrack.*

American Idol Rewind

Fame and fortune were her goals
Way beyond her, truth be told
Dreams, like ice, had melted down
Then the Preacher came to town

Now she more than entertains you
Empty hearts on every church pew
Respond to her beck and call
To embrace Him, one and all

Saved from vain imaginings, she sings
Praises to her King of kings
True riches have become hers, too
Despite the works she didn't do

Still, she labors till He comes
Sings yet to His different drum
Forgets all that she's left behind
All because He changed her mind

Writing Exercise
Lori Higgins
Prompt: *Write about reluctance or eagerness. (Bonus points if you can work them into the same short piece!)*

A Hope for the Future

For as long as I can remember I've been told how I am supposed to act. From the way I am expected to dress to my conduct whether in a group or by myself, it has all been laid out before me. I have done well enough, I suppose, but now it is all I can do not to protest, not to beg my father and brother not to go. Yet, I cannot. It would not make a difference. It has been planned for months and demanded by the King himself. Father even took the time to be sure I knew how to keep the manor running smoothly in his absence. I could do it in my sleep.

Knowing I must stay behind and wait—for news of their health or demise—weighs me down like a heap of sand. However, I lean into a promise that causes a flicker of hope. Once they both return, I will become a wife, and my chosen husband has promised I will be able to visit here as often as I want. My life, though planned, will begin in a new way, and the future awaits. I just must overcome the difficulties that are coming first. Surely then everything else will fall into place.

Writing Exercise
Patti Jarrett
Prompt: *Write about time.*

The Fugitive

    Minutes tick by, the chase is on, and once again, time escapes—slipping from my grip. Who holds the key that locks the door of the holding cell? Who can stop time in its tracks?
    Could it be the time-saving apps on my phone? Ha! We are only fooling ourselves. Often I've sought to contain those elusive moments, only to be slowed by the parade of paperless communications, missed messages, email extravaganza, and Facebook frolics. Tick. Tick. Tick.
    Maybe I'll take the battery out of the clock.

HAIKU

Struggling to make time

Bombarded by excuses

Finally, I sit.

Writing Exercise
Samuel Frech
Prompt: *Write about a day in the life of a superhero.*

Superhero

Woke up, flew to Japan, found a private bath house to relax in to start the day. Flew to the sun to dry off and explore the galaxy. Found we are not alone in this universe after all. There are others like us. Some have more issues. Some are in complete peace. Over all, I like where I am in the universe. There are problems I can help solve, but, in most cases, I can watch over everyone and enjoy being Invincible.

Writing Exercise
Ed Frost [†]
Prompt: *Write about waiting.*

Full of Bacon

Weighting? Is that like the butcher holding his thumb on the scale while he is weighing out your lamb chops? Maybe it's putting sandbags in the back of your pickup after a deep snow. Or, I suppose, it could be adding weight to the hook with the bacon on it to get to the 6-foot gray shark faster (after all, if he is full of bacon, perhaps he won't eat the kids, Andy!).

In my case, weighting is what I do when I get on the scale at the doctor's office—well, maybe that's de-weighting since I take everything out of my pockets including the lint.

Personally, I am not in favor of homonyms.

[†]Posthumous

Writing Exercise
Pam Piccolo
Prompt: *Write about the cold.*
For this exercise, the author responded in a variety of styles including a list (she's a researcher at heart) and a poem.

Baby, It's Cold Outside!

1. Bitter cold
2. Blood ran cold
3. Bone-chilling cold
4. Catch cold
5. Cold and calculating
6. Cold as iron
7. Cold as the tomb
8. Cold brew
9. Cold calling
10. Cold cash
11. Cold cereal
12. Cold cock
13. Cold comfort
14. Cold conditions
15. Cold drink
16. Cold feet
17. Cold fish
18. Cold hands
19. Cold hard facts
20. Cold light of day
21. Cold locker
22. Cold metal
23. Cold rain
24. Cold reality
25. Cold reception
26. Cold shiver of fear
27. Cold shoulder
28. Cold shower
29. Cold snap
30. Cold sober
31. Cold soup
32. Cold stare
33. Cold statistics
34. Cold storage
35. Cold sweat
36. Cold to the touch
37. Cold turkey
38. Cold water
39. Cold weather
40. Cold wind
41. Cold-blooded
42. Cold-hearted
43. Common cold
44. Freezing cold
45. Ice cold
46. In cold blood
47. Knew her stuff cold
48. Knocked out cold
49. Left me cold
50. Left out in the cold
51. Love of many grow cold
52. Performed the solo cold
53. Ran hot and cold
54. Scent went cold
55. Shivering cold
56. Stone cold
57. Stopped them cold
58. Throw cold water on it
59. Trail went cold
60. Turned down cold

237

Writing Exercise
Pam Piccolo
Prompt: *Write about the cold.*

The Coldest Place On Earth

The coldest place on earth
Is not far from the sun
Unwelcoming and hard
Love's beckoning undone

It's gradual at first
This rotating of the shoulder
Through every storm, defiant
This place grows cruel and colder

If Antarctica or Arctic
Was your thinking at the start
There are places colder still
Within the human heart

But seasons change through turning
And winter becomes spring
So does the heart through yearning
Seek rest from suffering

And in both cases true
It's as sure as death and taxes
The Son can shine on you
As sure as earth tilts on its axis

Writing Exercise
Dylan West
Prompt: *Write about reluctance or eagerness.*

Reluctance

Children as young as seven are mining cobalt, lithium, and rare earth elements in Africa. They often aren't given masks, so toxic dust deposits in their lungs, risking permanent damage. Many of these metals go into making "green" technology and serve as permanent magnets for our various electric motors.

Only one type of motor requires no permanent magnet at all—a reluctance motor. Instead of magnets, which demand the lives of young miners and cost hundreds of dollars per kilogram, a reluctance motor uses a steel rotor.

Why not use reluctance motors exclusively, then? Because they don't make enough torque for applications like electric vehicles. But a seventeen-year-old boy in Florida has built a new type of synchronous reluctance motor that makes more torque than existing ones. For this discovery, he won $75,000 at a science and engineering fair last year.

He's waiting for his patent to be accepted. If it is, this seventeen-year-old might just help save the lives of seven-year-olds on another continent.

Writing Exercise
Lori Higgins
Prompt: *Write about digging a hole.*

From Here to Yesteryear

As usual, the movies have deceived us once again. The actors make it look so simple. A quick swing of the shovel into the ground, and then scoops of dirt easily form a huge pile. Alas, that's not the case for me. I honestly thought digging in the ground would be easier; it's just dirt after all. Well, compact dirt, that certainly makes a difference versus it being loose.

I drive the metal shovel in the ground once more, and this time I use my foot for a little more of a "harrumph." I'm rewarded by my shovel only sinking an inch more. I adjust my ballcap and squint at the sun above. I've been digging for what? About fifteen minutes? Maybe I am being a little too hard on myself when it comes to not having a nice hefty pile of dirt to show my work.

I cast my sights to the white metal box that sits to my right, and for just a moment I consider abandoning this whole project all together. But my children will be disappointed if I do. It's not every day we make a time capsule. To think of all their little treasures not being buried would cause so much disappointment. I pick up my water bottle and take a long sip before I toss it aside, and then try the shovel again. With the grit of my teeth and using all my strength, it breaks into the earth, the dirt giving way as it sinks fully into the ground. Finally, things are fully underway, and it won't be long until it's buried. At least I hope. But will time pass as fast as a movie? That's an answer I will give in about twenty years.

Writing Exercise
Patti Jarrett
Prompt: *It was just like in the movies.*

Family Vacation

Last week, we took a *Family Vacation.* Well, not the whole family, just the hubby and me. We didn't have Chevy Chase, sassy kids, Grandma rocking on the car roof, or a dog tied to the bumper. We didn't go to Wally World, either. I guess it wasn't like *that* movie.

We drove down the east coast, and as far as we could tell, didn't run into any *Aliens,* but we did see a couple of suspicious-looking *Men in Black.*

At a stopover in Myrtle Beach, we heard live music from an outdoor stage—it was *Elvis*! We purchased tickets to ride the Skywheel, and who do you suppose was right smack in front of us in line? Elvis! Just like in the movie—except we weren't in Hawaii. Or Acapulco. Or Las Vegas. Elvis has a double chin now. The black hair slicked back and the trademark sideburns were a dead giveaway, though.

On River Street in Savannah, every menu offered *Fried Green Tomatoes.* We saw a lot of magnolias, but none appeared to be *Steel Magnolias.* Those must have been *Gone With the Wind.*

Historic ports and battlefields are calm now, no sign of *The Blue and the Gray* who waged many battles during *The Civil War.*

You wouldn't find us at *Midnight in the Garden of Good and Evil,* but a few carefree days on our own schedule found us declaring *"It's a Wonderful Life."*

Writing Exercise
Pam Piccolo
Prompt: *Write a memoir for each age using just six words.*

Six-Word Memoirs

Expecting sane outcomes, she pressed on. (age 15)

At rope's end, she let go. (age 25)

He was there all the time. (age 45)

When self dies, He still lives. (age 75)

Rachel Plumley
Prompt: *Six Word Memoir—What I'm afraid of*

The mice in the cornfield (age 5)

Living on the farm forever (age 15)

Not having a backup boyfriend (age 25)

Forgetting my sparkle shoes on the cruise (age 55)

Misplacing my lipstick (age 85)

Eileen Frost
Prompt: *Six Word Memoir—Describing Your Life*

Auburn hair, green eyes, spirit flares. (age 5)

Guitar strings, heart sings, anticipation burns. (age 15)

Grey hair, calm eyes, embers glow. (age 61)

Silver hair, eyes close . . . smoke rises. (age 90)

Writing Exercise
Ed Frost †
Prompt: *Write about something gone with the wind.*

Gone With The Wind
Just for Miss Ev and with sincere apologies to Margaret Mitchell

A poem I sat to write but ere a word was penned
I found, to my chagrin, my thoughts were gone with the wind.
Alas, now what to do? I don't think Evelyn would buy
That my words had been stolen by Yankees, evil and sly.

The dog ate my homework seemed less than appropriate
And I didn't want to risk that she would expropriate
My seat in writers group henceforth and forevermore
I cringed at hearing her proclaim "Nevermore!"

I've got it, this excuse she will have to believe!
I swear my assignment I had achieved,
But that final act of Sherman's occupation
Caused my paper to burn in Atlanta's conflagration.

†Posthumous

Writing Exercise
Benton Hammond
Prompt: *Write about a sudden silence.*

A Sudden Silence

He was used to a lot of silences.

What wannabe comedian isn't used to the crickets when a joke doesn't land? The awkward silence full of shifting eyes and shifting feet. The bored eyes staring as if he is a stain on the sidewalk. Something to look at and step over, but not worth a second thought. He brought the wrong material for the wrong crowd. At least that awkward silence ends with either a sympathetic chuckle or a cleared throat.

There is that fun little silence when his parents ask if he is finally going to get a real job. That one is full of weariness from both parties. A tiring routine that wasn't funny the first time, but has to happen every time. He dreams of the day when he can fill that silence with an emphatic, "This *is* my real job." Until then, there is just the painful silence filled with ticking clocks and disappointed sighs.

There is the big sad silence of his apartment when he locks the door at the end of the day. No joyful pet. He can't afford those. No busy family. They live across the state, and he can only have so many of those fun conversations. No encouraging friends. They grew up, moved on, and got "real jobs." No laughing girlfriend. She left. No need for counting sheep when he can drift off to all the faults she had. Or he had. Doesn't matter. The lonely silence is deafening.

A particularly pointed silence follows him when he asks for an extension on repaying his loans. From the bank to the pawn shop, he always promises it will be the last time, and they hit him with the sound of sheer disbelief. Scratching pens, tapping fingers, unfriendly glares. Calculators, computers, and old-fashioned ledgers out to get him every time. Nothing he can do but accept the judgment in silence.

But the silence that hit him the hardest is the sudden one. The one he doesn't anticipate before it arrives. The quick little wheeze and then it's gone. Tank's on E. He meant to put another three gallons in the tank yesterday, but he forgot. He rests his forehead on his steering wheel. Is this it? Is this a metaphor for his life? Out of fuel and out of gas?

No.

A quick prayer, and he hits the ignition. The brave little Mazda coughs and whines and wheezes back to life. There are still a few drops in the system, and he is not done yet. The gas station is within sight, and, if he hurries, he can still get to the comedy club with seconds to spare.

Writing Exercise
Rachel Plumley
Prompt: *Advice to a writer who is struggling*

Dear Younger Me

    Just write all the juicy, messy, horrible secrets! Then you won't have to think about them anymore.
    Pin the ghosts down on paper. They'll stick there and can't float around inside your head.
    Dig for details like treasure—they'll make your story sparkle! (Thanks for this, Dylan West.)
    Mine your mind for truth. Like the belt of truth, it holds everything together. (Love this idea from Patricia Shirer's *Prince Warriors*.)
    Finally, take breaks to walk around the block. Bird's song and flower's cheer is inspiration!

Writing Exercise
Dylan West
Prompt: *Write about a history of whispers.*

Ventifacts

In the Desert of Ventifacts, mutterings drift on the wind. Subtle tones shift into solid words in the ear of a Whisper Sage. These mushroom stones, with their wind-flattened faces, repeat the death rattles of all who fell in the desert and never rose again, as if Nature preserved those final cries as warnings to others. Men who seek the bones of Eden, the learned who trace the old course of the River Gihon to this very valley. In their wisdom, they found the land where paradise once grew. In their folly, they dig for what remains of it.

My people walk in the heat of noon without fainting. We hum in time with the wind to draw water from the sand. And we know not to exhume what earned its lonely slumber. For though the Garden died long ago, the Tree of Life did not. Its very nature is to live on forever. It rests in a cavern far below these sands. A chamber carved by the Flood and sealed off from questing hands that once plundered its great arboreal neighbor. That tree rests in its own cave and feeds knowledge to the wind. It is that knowledge I tap into now. That knowledge teaches me to live in the harshest land and guide would-be questors to safety. Or else carry their bodies to the village for our priests to bury with the others whose ears were plugged to the warnings on the wind.

If armed men approach, my sword is swift and strong. I spark it into flame with an oily breath and drive away all comers, just as my fathers did before me.

Writing Exercise
Patti Jarrett
Prompt: *Write about a mask.*

Just the Facts

My name is Patti and I am not a writer. Not a creative writer, anyway. Just the facts, ma'am. Cut and dry.

Julia Cameron might take me to task as I forego foraging artist dates and become remiss about morning pages.

My daughter, Queen of the Used Book Sales, loaned me a copy of *The Sound of Paper,* another offering from the aforementioned author. It's beckoning to me from the bookshelf after being banished for, let's just say, a *while* now, and was recently rediscovered.

I noticed a bookmark between the pages. The title page, introduction, etc., already read. It marked the first exercise. OK! I can do this!

The lesson spoke of a pearl, brought forth by the "interruption of equilibrium that creates beauty." Julia described her frustration after writing for 35 years. She wasn't writing, and not going to write! She found another way to cozy up to words—binge-reading—just to see what her writing friends were up to. One of them had sworn off writing. Julia noted that nothing gets a writer more off-center than not writing, and she had certainly sounded crabby about her high-minded decision to "just be a person."

Maybe I'm only a collector of writing paper, journals, fountain pens, and ink. But here I am, reading *The Sound of Paper,* starting from scratch—the scratch of a fountain pen nib on paper.

Writing Exercise
Karen McSpadden
Prompt: *Write about an end.*

On a June Night

At the bottom of the brick steps
the firefly is dying.
I don't know why.
I can't help.
I can't bring my heel down
to crush its last light
even if it would be mercy.
All I can do is walk beside the dog
into the dark
and list the things that are most beautiful
at the end:
Sunsets.
Embers.
Autumn.
The blue in your eyes
when you said
It's fine. We'll make it.
We'll be okay.

Writing Exercise
Ed Frost [†]
Prompt: *What does "beauty will save the world" mean to you?*

Beauty Triumphs

Even in war, God pushes the flowers up through the mud, the grime, the blood spilt on the ground. No matter what we as a people do, God—who is the ultimate beauty—triumphs.

[†] Posthumous

About the Authors

Photography by DM Frech

Ann ABRAHAM

Ann grew up in Indiana and received her bachelor's degree in communication from Taylor University, where she was editor of the university's student newspaper and alumni magazine. She worked in media communication for The Family Channel, The Virginian Pilot, and WHRO Public Media. Currently, she is a freelance writer and editor ghostwriting a client's memoir. Ann's writing has been featured in magazines, newspapers, newsletters, technical journals, advertising, and social media. She enjoys writing stories that convey honest messages of life and hope. A longtime member of the KPC Writers Group, Ann recently ventured into writing fiction, with several works in progress, including a novel and screenplay. She lives in Virginia Beach.

Olivia ARNEY

Olivia Arney grew up in Virginia Beach, VA. She completed her first novel when she was 17. An early high-school graduate, she attended Tidewater Community College, graduating in 2023. She is currently attending Regent University. After earning a bachelor's degree in English, she intends to continue writing and editing. Olivia has written several short stories, memoirs, poems, and published articles for her school paper.

James R. BOYD

James began writing poetry in 1975 to express the frustrations of living in Chicago. While in a course for creative writing, he wrote a short story, "The Old Man and the Bus Driver," that was published in the *Garland Court Review*. He was drafted, served in the U.S. Navy for 21 years, followed by a second career as a healthcare executive for the Commonwealth of Virginia. Still serving today, James is an ordained minister and Director Emeritus of a local Bible college. He has written hundreds of sermons, ministry training classes, and monthly prayer focus guidelines for a national prayer ministry. Publications include, "Public Health: The Next Battlefield" (AAMA Executive Fall 2003, Chicago, IL); "Aging Warrior" (Garland Court Review, Chicago, IL, 2013); "Seven Years" (*Garland Court Review*, Chicago, IL, 2015); *Special Forces Christians—The Rise of Militant Faith* (2016, Xulon Press).

Derick CARSTENS

Derick was born and raised in coastal Virginia. He is as old as his tongue and slightly older than his teeth. His parents (who were the greatest ever—fight him if you want), Dirk and Dianne, fostered in him a love for art, a compassion for people, and a sense of curiosity. They were his guiding lights until they went to be with Jesus. Derick's Savior pulled him out of some really dark places and has been with him through everything. Derick owes Him his life and his gratitude. His aim is to reflect Jesus to the world the best he can. With his creativity and curiosity, Derick hopes to draw people towards wanting to know Him. He currently writes fiction and poetry and can be reached at sevendaysastonished@gmail.com.

Billie
MONTGOMERY/COOK

Billie Montgomery/Cook is a proud graduate of Spelman College (BA, History) and Bowling Green State University (MA, College Student Personnel). She is the author of four books: the national bestseller *The Real Deal: A Spiritual Guide for Black Teen Girls* and *Sisters of Scripture: Mentors in Womanhood* (both published by Judson Press and winner of the "2016 Silver Illumination Award for Devotionals," the Jenkins Group); a historical fiction novel, *Georgiana Scott: A Free Child of Portsmouth*, and *Rise Up and Pray: Sustenance for A Pandemic, The 2020 Presidential Election and Beyond* (Amazon). She has written and presented a trilogy of plays based on the history of African Americans in the City of Portsmouth (Grant, VA Foundation for the Humanities/

VFH); and she has a line of drama ministry presentations, *There's Some Drama Up In Here*, with P-Town Books, her publishing company. Additionally, she is the Creative Director of The Not-Just-for February Players, her local African-American Readers Theatrical troupe based in Portsmouth, VA.

Presently, Cook serves as a freelance writer for *Having Church* magazine and as a contributing author/consultant for writers conferences and workshops, as well as a mentor/coach for budding writers and church drama ministries. She and her husband of 40+ years, Keith, are retirees; residents of Portsmouth, VA, and members of the historic Ebenezer Baptist Church. Booking and contact info: billiecook130@gmail.com; www.billiemcook.com.

Kathy DAUGHERTY

Kathy began writing at an early age and continued throughout her travels around the country as a Navy wife, including a tour in Guam. She specializes in devotionals and in using humor to drive home her point. Since 2001, she has served as the Prayer Liaison at a large church in Virginia Beach, VA, where she lives.

Sherry ELLIOTT

Sherry writes fiction and inspirational messages. She enjoys walks on the beach and listening to the roar of the ocean. She lives in Chesapeake, VA, with her husband. They have two adult children. Visit her upcoming blog at abideinyou.com.

Valerie FAY

Valerie was born and raised in England, where her love of the written word was nurtured. It started in school with a focus on classic English literature and historical novels. Valerie moved to the US in her early twenties, and for several years this interest took a back seat to raising a family. The desire to write was awakened along with an opportunity to teach the Bible soon after coming to know the Lord. Today, her love for God's Word and a passion to express truth in ways that reach the hearts of others leads her to write. Valerie focuses on writing Bible studies and devotionals, although she dabbles in other areas.

DM FRECH

DM Frech completed a BFA and MFA in dance at New York University, Tisch School of the Arts. After a career in modern dance, she moved to Virginia, was a stay-home mom, and later became a Realtor. She is a member of the KPC Writers Group, The Muse Writers, Hampton Roads Writers, Poetry Society of VA, Writers Guild of Virginia, The Virginia Writers Club, James River Writers, and AWP. She is an award-winning author who writes poetry, picture books, fiction, non-fiction, screenplays and is an avid photographer.

Finishing Line Press recently published her chapbooks: *Quiet Tree* and *Words From Walls* available through FLP, Amazon, and Barnes & Noble. Her work is also in *Streetlight Magazine*, *New Feather Anthology*, *WayWords Literary Journal*, *The Journal* of The Writer's Guild of Virginia, *Burningword Journal*, *Poets Choice*, *Writer's Journal* and *Bangalore Review*.

She has much gratitude for her father, Steven Kasmauski, who served in the military for 42 years. His unconditional love is felt years after his passing. And to her sons, Andrew and Samuel Frech, who inspire her daily to leave the swamp and climb the mountain. DM hugs trees and walks the earth by the grace of God.

Samuel FRECH

Samuel is an Norfolk Christian Schools alumnus, attended Tidewater Community College, shifted gears, and taught snowboarding and skiing for eight years at Snowshoe in WV, Beaver Creek/Vail, CO, and Whitefish, MT. He left the mountains to help his father. Presently, he is a barista at Starbucks, writes, and is an avid photographer. His art photograph, "Pointing Tree," is published in the Spring 2024 *New Feathers Anthology*.

Ed FROST

Ed was born on an island in the middle of Tampa Bay and was convinced that contributed to his "slightly off-kilter" personality. He grew up in a military family under the "manners, language, and woodlore" of his Aunt Sue and then joined the Navy himself. Eventually his adventures charted a course to his beloved wife Neelie and to a second career as a logistics engineer. Ed wrote for fun and for his friends. When he wasn't writing, he could be found reading, woodburning, spending time with his grandchildren, and annoying Neelie. He went to be with his Savior in 2022. Though he is greatly missed, his writing continues to enrich our lives.

Eileen FROST

Eileen, graced with a Walter Mitty imagination ever since she was a young girl, saw a story almost everywhere she looked. She wrote great first liners that didn't always go any further but were lots of fun to play with. She later moved to poetry and rhyming stories. Having work published online encouraged Eileen greatly, and she has since written several short stories. Her favorite, "The Poppy and the Raven," was originally written for children but has proven to be a life message for all ages.

Elizabeth GREEN

Elizabeth writes children's books, curriculum, and poetry. Her vision is to write so that lives will be transformed for the glory of God. During her teaching career in Norfolk Public Schools, she became passionate about teaching students to write. Elizabeth has two adult children and lives in Suffolk, VA. Her children's book titles include, *Candy Girl, Seven Days and Seven Prayers with Prayer Journal, Set of Bible Story Posters with Curriculum Guide,* and *Wee Disciples* (new release, 2024). Dr. Green is the founder of Green Pastures Publishing, LLC, and Kidz Write For Kidz, Inc.

Joyce HAMMER

Joyce is a former elementary education teacher and Regent University Library Service Clerk. She currently works at Bracha Hair Salon as a receptionist and lives with her husband, Bob, in Chesapeake, VA. Joyce and Bob committed their lives to Jesus Christ in 1974. Joyce has served as an editor and is currently co-writing a book about God's grace and mercy.

Benton HAMMOND

Benton has believed from a young age that fiction writing is his calling. He looks forward to publishing his magnum opus one day. In the meantime, he enjoys working at a TV station, as well as producing music and drawing comics.

Amy HEILMAN

Amy found creative writing to be her favorite subject in grade school. In college, writing became her greatest outlet for self-processing and expression. Moving into adulthood, writing became a passion that led to her first published book, *Soul Stripper, Confessions by One Ex-Pastor's Wife*. She loves reading and writing to inspire the soul and one's spiritual formation rooted in the Living Word. Amy finds joy in being out in God's creation and spending quality time with family and friends where she resides in the beauty of Virginia.

Lori HIGGINS

Lori has loved stories for as long as she can remember. When she is not working or daydreaming about her current story, she tends to find herself lost in reading. Currently, she is writing her first novel, a historical romance set in 12th-century England. Lori resides in Chesapeake, VA, with her husband, Michael, and their three children.

Penny HUTSON

Penny began her writing career as a newspaper reporter at the tender age of 17. After college, she became an English teacher and, later, a school librarian for both middle and high school students. Now retired, she spends her days writing, quilting with friends, and traveling with her husband. They live in Virginia Beach, VA.

Patti JARRETT

Patti's writing menu includes journaling, devotional, and memoir, often served with a dollop of humor. Nature lovers at heart, she and her husband live the retired life exploring their surroundings in Virginia and beyond.

Joyce KIRBY

Joyce, a grateful believer in Jesus Christ, lives in Norfolk, VA, with her husband, Jamie. She writes devotions, prayers, and poetry to encourage others in their personal Christian walk. She is a member of King's Choir of Hampton Roads. In addition to writing and singing, she enjoys traveling, reading, and watercolor painting.

Karen McSPADDEN

Karen writes fiction and poetry from Virginia Beach, Virginia, where she lives with her husband, her three girls, and any number of overstuffed bookshelves. When she's not writing, she can be found on the beach, in her local yarn store, or on the hunt for a good cup of tea.

Merle MILLS

As a young girl, Merle began writing poems for special occasions, such as Mother's Day and birthdays, and to encourage friends who were going through difficult situations. She also journaled, a practice she continues and that helps her look back and compare the tremendous growth that continues to take place in her life. She has authored five devotional books: *No More A Secret: Poems, Prayers, and Promises: A Guide to Healing After Abortion*, *You are Forgiven*, *Who Are You?*, *Hand In Hand With the Master*, and *You Can Choose to Say No*. She maintains a weekly blog (changedthrutheword.org). Merle resides with her family in Virginia Beach, VA.

Jennifer NAPIER

Jennifer is a storyteller, an eclectic writer of inspirational devotionals, poetry, short stories, and cozy mysteries that reveal beauty, humor, and help make sense of life's difficulties. An extensive reader, she is also a mother of five, crafter, homeschooling mom, and entrepreneur based in Chesapeake, VA. Her writings can be found on www.musingsbyjennifer.blogspot.com. Her first cozy mystery will be coming out next year.

Jayne ORMEROD

Jayne is a multi-published author who writes coastal cozies with a splash of humor. She grew up in a small Ohio town and attended a small-town Ohio college. Upon earning her accountancy degree, she became a CIA (that's not a sexy spy thing, but a Certified Internal Auditor). She married a naval officer, and off they sailed to see the world. After 19 moves, they, along with their two rescue dogs, settled in a cottage by the Chesapeake Bay. Jayne writes what she knows: small towns with beach settings. You can read more about Jayne and her many publications at www.JayneOrmerod.com.

Pam PICCOLO

Pam is a charter member of the KPC Writers Group and has served as alternating guest speaker/admin support since 2006 for ladies retreats ministering to the mid-Atlantic region, as well as women's ministry "Maturity Base Coach," prayer ministry leader, and praise team vocalist. More researcher than storyteller, her primary focus has nevertheless been narrative nonfiction, using humor and ancestral anecdotes highlighting her Italian heritage to make deep spiritual truths accessible via devotionals, Bible studies, and memoir. Pam is combining all three approaches in her current book project, *Funny Little Man/Funny Little Woman*, addressing biblical masculinity/femininity from a lighthearted perspective. An accompanying cookbook of family recipes might even be in the works, an inescapable addition given her ethnic background. Pam lives in Chesapeake, Virginia, with Jack, her pony-tailed, musically-inclined husband of 43 years.

Sherrie PILKINGTON

Sherrie enters into various aspects of life, first as a daughter of the One True God. She dearly loves her two grown sons and two "daughters-in-love," but it's her six grandchildren who bring the joy in her laughter and keep her young at heart. Known for pondering the hard things in life through the lens of God's heart, Sherrie shares her revelations through her podcast, *Finding God in Our Pain.* Sherrie and her guests do not shy away from the difficult questions about the reality of pain and suffering and the good God we profess. After unexpectedly losing her husband in early 2018, whom she had been with for a little over 33 years, she now knows that God speaks beautiful things in the dark. Through her website (alifeofthrive.com) and her podcast, Sherrie proclaims that we are never alone in our pain, because God enters into the darkest of valleys and will gently shepherd us through.

Rachel PLUMLEY

Rachel Plumley is a writer and graphic designer. She is published as an editor and designer of *The Student Worldview Dictionary*, a student's edition of Webster's 1828 *Dictionary*. After studying at Liberty University and Regent University, she worked for a decade at the Foundation for American Christian Education where she learned book layout and design. She writes poetry and is currently working on her memoir. She travels America with her Coast Guard husband and three boys.

John REDDEL

John began his writing career working on screenplays in film school. This turned into a career in television video production at the Christian Broadcasting Network (CBN), where he has written everything from children's shows to commercial scripts. He is currently working on two middle-grade fantasy fiction novels and several short stories. He enjoys the day-to-day adventures of trying to keep up with his two redheaded daughters and his very social wife.

Yvonne SAXON

Yvonne enjoys writing for the young at heart. A former classroom teacher and librarian, her interests include reading, research, puzzles, coffee, and mysteries of all kinds. She lives in Chesapeake, VA, with her family and a very tiny, but temperamental cat. Three short stories have been published in the anthologies *Virginia is for Mysteries*, Volumes I, II, and III. She is currently working on her first novel.

Jessica SNOOK

Jessica's writing includes poetry, devotionals, fantasy fiction, and humor. Her poem "Essence of Learning," is published in the anthology *Things I Know Now*. She is working on her second novel. Her day job as a Nurse Practitioner supports her creative lifestyle of writing, knitting, martial arts, and Middle Eastern dance.

Mary STASKO

Mary enjoys research and writes non-fiction, poetry, and journal entries. She started writing in high school and, except for a break now and then, has never stopped. Her faith guides her in her writing, and her goal is to be published in the next year or two. She hopes this anthology inspires you to get your writing out there!

Julie STROHKORB

Julie is a certified K-6 teacher, writer, and creative advocate for children. She lives in Houston, TX, where she designs many of her own educational materials. Julie enjoys the art of the advanced organizer, the simplicity of the sock puppet, and the spark of inspiration when collaborative writing with kids.

Evelyn J. WAGONER

In addition to inspirational romance novels, poetry, and nonfiction, Evelyn writes "Love Stories" for entertainers to present at wedding receptions, edits manuscripts, mentors fellow writers, and has led the KPC Writers Group in Virginia Beach, VA, since its inception in May 2004. She is a member of American Christian Fiction Writers (ACFW) and Hampton Roads Writers (HRW), where she serves on the advisory board.

Having won several short story and poetry awards, Evelyn was thrilled to find *The Kulwicki Chronicles*, her tribute to Winston Cup champion Alan Kulwicki, on display in the NASCAR Hall of Fame in Charlotte, NC. Her debut novel, *The Canary Cage*, was published by Elk Lake in 2019 and has received a significant number of five-star reviews. Evelyn lives happily in Virginia Beach, VA, with Rod, her amazing husband and staunchest supporter. www.evelynjwagoner.com

Steven D. WEBBER

Steven's desire to illustrate a dynamic relationship with Father God germinated after joining a Christian group committed to high schoolers. This grew into mentoring students at a military academy, where he wrote to continue nurturing those who had moved on from the academy. Over the past four decades, he has joined many in traveling through a season of their lives—as a friend, coach, counselor, or just "Pop."

In 2022, he organized his experiences of learning to forgive into book and audio form. Currently, Steven lives with Barnabas, his Aussie shepherd, in Chesapeake, VA. As his life crosses paths with others, he is endeavoring to practice His presence.

Dylan WEST

Dylan is a Jesus lover, web developer, Navy vet, foreign language nut, and a nut in general. While other people are busy thinking normal thoughts, he's crafting corny jokes. Dylan is the author of the *Scribes* Series, and the developer of the related video game, "Scribes' Descent." He lives with his wife and daughter in Chesapeake, VA. Free samples of his game and books are available on his website: https://dylanwestauthor.com

Acknowledgements

We would first like to thank and acknowledge Marshele Carter Waddell, author of *Hope for the Homefront*. Her simple question, "Do you belong to a writers group?" asked across a pew at Saturday night church, was the impetus for the formation of the KPC Writers Group back in 2004. While she was unable to remain with the group more than a couple of months, we are grateful that she recognized the need for a writing community and got us started.

Thanks to Reverend Neil Ellison, KPC's Congregational Care pastor, who oversaw the church's Life/Small Groups. He agreed we had a great idea and served as our sponsor for many years. What a surprise to learn he could write more than sermons and devotionals and had a love for drama, adventure, and plot twists!

Thanks to Valerie Fay for her creativity and generous contribution of her talents. Valerie never fails to deliver whether she's asked to design a bookmark or a book cover for the group. We love and appreciate her more than we can express (which is a tough thing for writers to admit!)

Thanks to Rachel Lyons Plumley for countless hours spent designing and formatting the beautiful interior layout. Her sweet spirit and willingness to juggle varying points of view and suggestions made the arduous pre-publication process a joy when left in her competent hands.

Thanks to our editing and proofing team: Ann Abraham, Karen McSpadden, Jayne Ormerod, Rachel Plumley, Pam Piccolo, and Evelyn Wagoner, and to all the authors who so enthusiastically supported and contributed to this anthology. It is our prayer that faith-based writers everywhere will find encouragement and delight within its pages.

Many thanks to Evelyn, whose vision began over twenty years ago and whose creative fortitude, propelled by her love of writing and her compassion for writers, keeps the group active and charged. Her soulful humor and perseverance planted a mecca for Christian writers. This anthology bears one of its many fruits.

And, finally, we are grateful to the Kempsville Presbyterian Church staff who has supported our group's ministry for all these years. We couldn't survive without you.

Made in the USA
Middletown, DE
26 November 2024